OMG What a Mistake
~STARTING OVER AFTER A BAD RELATIONSHIP~

This is my story. All of the names, characters, places, organizations and events portrayed are the product of the author's personal experiences and any resemblance to actual persons, living or dead, businesses, incidents are solely coincidental.

Printed in the United States of America

All rights reserved. No part of this book may be stored or introduced into a retrieval system or transmitted, in any form, or by any means electronic, mechanical, or recording or used or reproduced in any manner whatsoever without written permission except in cases of brief quotations used in articles or reviews. The scanning, uploading, and distribution of this book via the Internet or via any other means without the publisher's permission is illegal and punishable by law.

ISBN -13: 978-1-4840-3500-9

Mica Callaway, LLC
P.O. Box 312064
Atlanta, GA 31131

Book cover design and inside layout by www.mariondesigns.com

OMG! What a Mistake: Starting over after a bad relationship
By Mica Callaway

© 2013 Mica Callaway, LLC

Dedications

I want to first dedicate this book to my first love Jesus Christ. My grandfather the late Cleophues 'GUE' Mitchell, my grandmother Betty A Mitchell, My father the late Theodore Richardson and my mother Deborah Monroe, my children and all the Wonderful Spiritual Leaders and teachers who played a major role in the development of the woman I am today. A Wonderful change has come over me.

    I dedicate this book to the night before Thanksgiving in 2012. Tonight, through all my disappointment and pain, I will pour my spirit into this book as a release. Celebrating the last tear, I cried concerning a battle that the Lord has constantly told me he would fight for me. Ladies, I will share with you a living testimony, of why you should wait for Jesus to bring you a soul mate. I pray this is also encouragement for you to know how sovereign Jesus is in all of our lives, regardless of mistakes.

    Even though you make mistakes, God never makes a mistake; He is still taking you where you belong. And will get you back on track.

Forward

We all hate it when we make a mistake, especially one that could have been avoided. There is an old saying: "We live and we learn." Our obstacles help make us who we are. Life, decisions we make, and experiences we go through can make us dry and brittle....almost lifeless.

That is how I saw Mica in the beginning...a dry brittle thorny, almost lifeless branch.

With Mica being covered divinely, cultivated, and fertilized as she comes through adversity and the vicissitudes of life, her roots grow deep and strong. From time to time, I'm allowed to water (share the word) I'm allowed to pull a few weeds that creep up (praying, interceding and sharing insight). As time will have it, there was a transformation. There is a renewed strength about her flexibility ....no longer brittle. No longer just a branch, but a bush with many branches. A bush that has produced a fruit, this writing *OMG! What a Mistake.*

This book will provide a behind the scenes view. No matter where you are, whether it's dry, brittle, almost lifeless, or being cultivated and pruned; you will be a "covered branch" becoming a bush, with fruit and many other buds to bloom.

By Mary K. Sheppard ~Spiritual Mother Kathy~

Chapters

1. My Story- Gods Favor
2. 30-N Ticking
3. I'ma Save Him
4. Drama 911
5. It's Over
6. IV-Giveness
7. #1stLOVEFoCuS
8. Testimony

Chapter 1
My Story: Gods Favor

Since my birth, I knew Jesus but as most of us say, "I grew up in the church". I had a great grandmother that was on the mother board and wore white every Sunday. I had aunts in the choir and even had my name engraved on a pew. With that being said, I was still living a life that was not totally surrendered to the Lord. At a certain age I knew pre-marital sex was wrong and a sin, but I still did it. At 15 years old I was pregnant. Yes me the "church girl", but please don't judge me. Jesus allowed that pregnancy to end through an ectopic (tubal) pregnancy. Now as an adult, I reflect back at the situation as a blessing and Jesus protecting me.

By the time I had finished high school, I had already smoked marijuana, had pre-marital sex, and stole the car out of the driveway on many nights to chase after a boy. But I always showed up at church on Sunday, looking cute and of course "growing up in the church". But how many of you know that at that time the church was not growing up in me.

I had a very good life being raised by my grandparents and knowing both my parents. I had the opportunity to know both of my great grandmothers as well. All of my life, my grandparents showed favoritism towards me, even though I was one of 13 grandchildren. They always said, "Because I was raised in their house, I was one of their children." I always wished they would treat all the grandchildren the same, so I would not feel like an outcast or the favorite. They both raised me very well, but I spent a lot of quality time with my grandpa. I called him "daddy". He was the best example a girl could have as a father figure. He tried his best to always treat everybody equal. I say this to say, I had a great male role model in my life and his opinion mattered. He had strong Christian beliefs and he followed the Bible saying: "Train up a child in the way that they shall go, and they will never depart from it". Now that he is gone to glory, I sit and reminisce over things that he would say to me. It all makes sense now that I'm all alone and relying on Jesus, without my grandfather to call or lean on. He would say things like:

"Don't stretch yourself too thin" with regards to finances

"You need to know the difference between priorities and necessities"

"Don't wait till it's too late" when I needed help

He had that seasoned wisdom. He always communicated with me, and we could talk about any and everything. He knew about my intimate life, finances, school, and boys. My friends loved him too and also called him grandpa. He was my favorite guy. By having this consistent example, I knew I would be equipped with the tools to find a great husband, well at least I thought. I remember when my high school boyfriend and I would have our differences, my grandpa would say, "That boy gone be the death of you!" If I did something wrong and did not tell the truth he would say, "A parent knows their child and I know you did it because I know you." and "The truth will go further than a lie." He never condoned my wrong and always steered me back in the right position, just like Jesus. I know he is looking down on me, while his angels encamp all around me and give me peace in a storm. I thank him so much for the Godly foundation which I had rooted and grounded in me at a small age. He taught me about morals, values and most importantly responsibility. If you are reading this book and you have a father that is still living, give them a hug, phone call and/or reach out to them and thank them for just allowing you to know who they are. Forgive them if they have not been a great example and love them in spite of their shortcomings, because some fathers can only do the best that they know how to. But the God we serve is a Father to the fatherless, and He is able to heal and comfort you. So, if you don't know who your father is, get to know Jesus and you will realize He will fill the void.

By the time I graduated from high school, my grandfather said in love, "You got two options: work or go to school, but you can't stay here and do nothing". I prepared to go to college and all I knew was that I was getting far away from home. I decided to go to Southern University because I had close family friends that are like cousins to me that attended school there. My family and church members saw me off to college. By now, I had a mentor and spiritual mother at the church. So of course, I had the student bible with a personal message on the inside and a spiritual calendar. I was surrounded by the word all the time.

Now, I'm on new territory in Baton Rouge, LA at Southern University. I'm a freshman now, living in a dorm room that's far away from home with no parents, grandparents, or church. All I now know is parties and boys with no chaperon. The church bus would come pick-up the students on Sunday mornings and I would attend often, but not on a regular basis because I was far away from home.

Now I'm officially a mid-west girl living in the "dirty south". It took time to get adjusted to the differences and allowed me to see life in a different aspect. A lot of things were different now and took some getting used to. Everything from their food to their style of dress. The way that they talk was different from anything that I had ever seen or heard before. In the mid-west we say, "I'm going to go buy groceries." In the south they would say, "We going to go make groceries." I'm thinking to myself, "Okay the groceries are already made. All you have to do is purchase them."

It did not take long for me to get adjusted though. I met new friends, M Keough from The Bay area, Elvern Cooks from Pine Bluff, Arkansas, and Mia Reid from Atlanta, GA. My freshman year Mia and I were really close. We did everything together good, bad and ugly. If you couldn't find us on campus, we were up front in the football dorms. Sophomore year, Mia did not return because she loved Atlanta too much. Soon I was going home with friends like Mert Rolando Franklin to small towns that are not even on the map like Greensburg, LA. I'm eating crawfish, something I had never seen in my life and enjoying it. So of course, I'm having fun and kicking it. So I met this guy from Greensburg, LA, and since my friend is from there, I conveniently went home with her often just to see him. I see him on the campus of Southern University, so I assumed he was a college student. I went to a party in Greensburg one weekend and decided to go to his house afterwards. I was not the girlfriend and sex does not mean commitment, which I did not know at the time. Now I'm 19 years old and pregnant. Not by my husband, nor by my boyfriend. I'm actually not even the other chick. It was just some random sex. Yep! The church girl is away at college getting a degree and gets pregnant. Now I'm calling on Jesus because I got to tell my grandparents and family that I'm pregnant. I don't really even know him. I have seen him three times and he has never taken me out on a date. He doesn't probably know Jesus and also I had no idea if he had AIDS or some incurable disease. Majority of what I know about him was what my friends had told me. I have heard his girlfriend was from Greensburg and lived on campus, but she lived up front in the honors dorms. When he would come to see me in the back dorms, she had no clue. I'm pregnant, OMG! WHAT A MISTAKE! I'm the church girl. I can't let anybody see me pregnant and not married. I'm in my second year of college, living in the sophomore dorms getting sick every day. Some days I just wanted my grandma and to go home. I also wanted to finish college at Southern University. After four months of pregnancy and getting sick every day the dorm mother said, "They could not be responsible for me." I had to withdraw from college and go home and face my grandparent's disappointment towards me for wasting their money and time. My grandmother would holler at me,"Ain't no baby coming in my house!" but my grandfather was supportive. Shortly after I returned home and got settled with a doctor, I began to go back to my home church, Christian Temple Baptist Church. I was 19 years old and pregnant, needing and wanting Jesus more in my life daily.

I was approached by an old saint in the church. She said, "You know you gone have to apologize to the church". I said, "Apologize to the church? For what?" She said, "Because you got pregnant out of wedlock". I said, "Well I'm not coming back to church because I'm not apologizing to anyone". She said, "If I had to do it, then you do too". I started that day to battle with my relationship with God. But I wanted to know for myself, what is the biblical approach for getting pregnant out of wedlock. I could not find anywhere in the Bible that indicated that I had to apologize to a congregation for my sin of getting pregnant out of wedlock. I realized that day that if you don't have a personal relationship with the Lord, you can be easily misled by an individuals' sense of doctrine. I wanted to understand more about denominations and the difference between religion and spirituality. I began to waver in my church attendance. I never really told anyone why or discussed what happened. So one Sunday, I came to church and this young minister, Pastor James, was preaching and the word was for me. I heard that he was a circuit preacher that preaches on first and third Sunday. The current pastor was getting close to retirement and was seeking a new pastor. I began to come to church only when the circuit preacher was scheduled to preach. As a 20 year old, at the time, I could relate to him. And as a former employee of the Boys and Girls Club, he could relate to the youth. I began to have my spiritual life challenged, about the type of music I listened to, and what I was coming in contact with in my spirit. I attended a small bible study that Pastor James started for me and two other young girls my age, because it was not too many young people at the church at that time. We became each other's accountability partners. Soon I became a mother at 20 years old to Shawn. My baby was a couple of weeks old, and I went back to work a week after she was born at AT&T. I was totally about my career and providing for her. Her father played his part in her life and soon wanted a relationship. My grandfather came from the old school. During his day, you stay with the woman which you have a child by and raise the child in a family environment. I explained to my grandpa, I left him when I was 4 months pregnant and "I don't like him like that" to be in a relationship. "Old school" grandparents could not understand that a woman did not want a relationship with a man she had a baby with. I informed them that it was just something that happened. Basically, I was not the same person I was when I first approached college. As a woman becomes a mother, everything changes as it relates to responsibility and providing. He could not see it. All he saw was a new mother disappointed in herself for not completing school and needing a way to accomplish her goals as a mother.

    I knew at a young age I wanted to be a dentist and/or have a career in dentistry. My grandfather played an important role in my life, and he always said its best to have a trade. I woke up one morning and went to apply for a trade as a dental assistant. My focus was not on a man at this moment in my life. I prayed for direction and began to remember scriptures and quote scripture in my prayer time, to bring things back to God's remembrance of what his word said. My relationship with my spiritual mother was stronger now, than prior to me going to college. I wanted more of Jesus. My mentor was my spiritual mother's sister and I had great relationships with both. I even had a great and wonderful godmother I could call on. But I wanted more of a challenge, and we all have different friends, we call for different things to get different results. We have the friend that will agree with us, and we have the friend that will just listen. I completed dental assistant school, obtained a trade, and began a career that I felt would assist me in providing for my daughter. My child's father has always done his part to the best of his ability with us being in different states.

By this time in my life, Shawn was growing up, and I was growing up as a mother and spiritually at the same time. I was pleasing my grandfather as a working mother, so he decided to bless me one day. He said, "Let's go look for you a car". I was so excited and my mentality was I don't want to break the bank. So I'm looking for used and inexpensive cars. My grandfather did not believe in foreign cars, so we went to the Ford dealership on Broadway. I left the dealership that day with my first car. It was a brand new car that had never been taken out of the plastic. The car had 8 miles on it and was a 1997 Ford Escort that just got delivered to the dealership. My grandfather co-signed for me and talked to me about establishing credit. His beacon score was so sharp that we didn't need a down payment to get the car. That day I learned the importance of credit and beacon scores. I want to have good credit like my grandpa, so I can purchase whatever I want. I will never forget the talk we had on the porch that evening. Again about necessities and priorities, and never stretch yourself too thin that you can't make it financially. We talked about 30-60-90 days late on the credit report. I was 20 years old and never looked at my credit report in my life. I obtained my credit report, to find that when I was in college at Southern University, someone had stolen my identity. I began to work on my credit to rebuild what had been stolen. Now everything seemed to be on track in my life. I was working and attending church on a regular. I was a new mother with a lot of good help and assistance from my family. My child's father was sending money monthly for childcare and assistance. I was working, going to school, paying my bills on time and working on my credit. Life was grand because I was still living at home with my grandparents without any financial responsibility.

My father, stepmother and brothers relocated to Atlanta, GA from Kansas City, MO. I never wanted to stay in Kansas City since I returned from Baton Rouge, LA. But I never knew where I wanted to relocate. I was contemplating on leaving when the time was right, and I heard from the Lord. I knew that the Lord had bigger plans for my life, beyond the capabilities of Kansas City. I was not afraid to step out on faith, since I kind of had to make it on my own in Baton Rouge, LA.

I and a close cousin decided to go the 2000 Super Bowl XXXIV in Atlanta, GA. We stayed with my step mother. At this time, my biological father has already died due to cancer. I can't explain how much fun we had in Atlanta that weekend. It was so serious that I did not want to get on the plane and go back to Kansas City. I lost my mind like I was in college again. I left Jesus on the sideline dugout and never let him up for bat that weekend. I told Jesus not to suit up. I was so amazed about all these wonderful black people. I also was 21 years old and being grown was not an option, it was understood. After that weekend in Atlanta, GA, I could not wait to get to Atlanta, GA on a fulltime basis. I prayed everyday about moving to Atlanta, GA. It seemed like a place that never slept and where all the successful black people live. I know God can find something for me to do in Atlanta, GA; a place where everything is happening all the time, even for black women and church girls like me. I was not able to establish boundaries with a good time on a Godly platform. I could not find out where the single, saved folks were having good clean fun at in Kansas City, Mo. But I thought to myself, I bet the church folks have their own thing going on in Atlanta, GA. I just got to find out where it is.

By August 2000, I was 23 years old, my daughter Shawn (3 years old) and I put our items in a car and drove to Atlanta, GA. I found a job prior to the move, which made it great to move with a job. I had a week prior to my first day of work. I used that week to learn my way around and get Shawn in a pre-school. I was blessed to live with my stepmother until I was able to get my own place. My grandpa told me to get a trade and it can work for my benefit. So, of course, my new job was as a dental assistant. I always wanted to complete my degree, so I also enrolled in school at Atlanta Metropolitan College. I had lost contact with Mia, my friend from Southern University, that was so in love with Atlanta, GA and I always wondered where she was. One day she called my grandmother because grandparent's phone numbers never change. She found out I was in Atlanta, GA and called me to my surprise. We reconnected like we never missed a day without each other. Now she was a single mother of a little girl, so our little girls bonded. We would help each other with the kids and work. My grandmother had a strong bond for Shawn, her great granddaughter. She insisted that Shawn stay in Kansas City with her until I got myself more settled in her opinion. So I took her up on the offer, until a later date. Mia introduced me to every hook up in Decatur, GA. Soon I had an apartment, was going to school, had a job, and was working a side hustle as a waitress at the strip club. Mia waitressed at Jazzy T's and I was a waitress at Pin-Ups. We were popping like college days but on a different level now. I loved Atlanta, GA just as much as Mia did now that I lived here every day. But no matter where I went, I always went to church and so did Mia. In Atlanta, I was exposed to leaving the club and going to church regardless. I would go out every single night and still made it to work on time the next morning. One night, I was solo at the Velvet room on Peachtree Street. I met this guy there. He was a local Georgia rapper named Hip-Hop. We exchanged numbers. The next day, I had a conversation with Mia about him. I said, "I met this guy last night and the weirdest thing is, that he had a wrestling belt on, but he said he's not a wrestler". She said, "Oh that is weird!" and I never said his name. Hip-Hop and I started to go out and have fun. So one night we decided to go around the corner to Jazzy T's where Mia was working. When we walked in the door of Jazzy T's, people were coming up to acknowledge him. It was so over whelming to me because I was like, "Who he thinks he is?" Mia came up to me and snatched me by my arm asking, "Are you with him?" I said, "Yes! Mia this is the guy I was telling you that wears the belt and is not a wrestler." So she was like, "Oh My God! You did not say his name. You always say my new guy friend." I said, "Well that's him. Who is he?" She told me he was a local rapper, but I had never heard of him in my life. Mia said, "They probably don't listen to him in Kansas City. He is a local rapper of Georgia." I said, "So if he is not big why are they acting like this?" She said, "He is big in the ATL." When we got back to my house, Hip-Hop explained that he liked my style and the fact that I did not know who he was attracted him to me. We maintained our dating relationship, to the point that I was going to all these small towns in Georgia. Where ever he had a concert I was with him. He would take me shopping to all of the outlet malls, and was such a gentleman to me. He made sure I had groceries and I would take him dinner at the studio. I even attended some baseball games at Ben Hill recreation with him. He always wanted me with him and the only place I did not like to go to was the Bounce. It was a ghetto, hood club on Bankhead.

In May 2001, I had a huge tragedy in my life. I received a phone call that my 14 year old baby brother, Gucci, had been killed and I had to rush home to Kansas City. That was the first time I wanted to be at home in a hurry and could not get there fast enough. The night prior, Hip-Hop and I were at the Velvet Room, on a Tuesday having fun celebrating where we met just kicking it. Things in life change overnight or in a twinkle of an eye. I got to Kansas City with my family, at such a tragic moment of my life, and the gentleman that Hip-Hop had appeared to be sent flowers. I stayed in Kansas City for a while, and throughout the day every attempt to reach him was futile. The person that I began to spend every day with had kind of vanished away. Now it was time to go back to Atlanta. I was thinking that we were going to start off where we finished, or maybe he would be a shoulder to cry on. By the time I got back to Atlanta, Hip-Hops number was not working. So I went to his house and then the studio and his brother was there alone. I asked his brother where he was. I had been looking for him. He said, "Just go home. He will reach out to you soon". I felt like something was wrong and weird, but decided just to go home like he said. I went to work the next day and I got a message from him to call him at a particular unknown number. I went to the break room, called the number and got a voicemail. There was a girl on the voicemail. I left a message, "Hello this is Hip-Hops girl. Can you please have him call me back? He just left a message and I'm concerned about him." I left my cell phone number. He soon called back to the job again and not my cell. I finally talked to him and asked whose phone it was since a girl was on the voicemail. He said it was his boy's phone and his girl on the voicemail. I asked where he was and he explained he needed to talk to me, and he would meet me at my house by a certain time. By the time I got off from work, I got a call on my cell phone from an unknown number. I answered and a girl says, "Can I speak to Mica?" I said, "Who is this?" She said, "This is Hip-Hops wife. How did you get this number?" I was stunned. I could not believe he was married because I used to be with him every day and night. We finally talked that evening and he explained himself to me. We soon ended the relationship or whatever we had. I thought to myself that that was a worthless mistake and a waste of time. I realized how I began to be exposed to different things and people in Atlanta, GA.

    I wanted Jesus for my mom's sake because she was hurting and grieving over the tragedy of losing my baby brother. He was her youngest child. My prayer life was not where it used to be, so I felt that I could not get a prayer through. I wanted Jesus for my sake because I could not believe I was dating a married man, without my knowledge. I wanted Jesus more and didn't want to work at the strip club anymore, even if I was just a waitress. Everybody just had too much going on in their lives. God was dealing with me about the way that I was living, and the people I was attracting into my life. I stopped working at Pin-Ups shortly after and moved to the Southside of town. I did not want any parts of Decatur, GA, strip clubs, married men, drama, or foolishness.

I changed my environment, and even though I was still in school, I pursued school harder to complete my degree. I started working at the Macy's in South DeKalb mall for seasonal help. It didn't bring in the money like the strip club, but the environment was better. I met this woman named Momma D. She always talked about her church and how much I reminded her of her daughter. I soon built a relationship with a church-going woman and not a strip club groupie. I was still attending school at night at Atlanta Metropolitan College. I met a new friend named Candace Crown. She introduced me to the word "sponsor", and anytime we went out, we had a "sponsor" to pay for it. She had a daughter that reminded me of Shawn, who was still with her great grandma. I began to miss Shawn so much in my life as it settled down. I began to calm down off of my "Atlanta high." I was not excited anymore about partying. I wanted to get my degree and career off of the ground to be a better mom. I wanted to be married and have a family. I began to go to Favor Baptist Church with Momma D. I really enjoyed Favor Baptist Church it was close to home at the time. The word was powerful and reminded me of Christian Temple Baptist Church in Kansas City, MO which was my home church. I always missed Pastor James word and wished it was not so far away. Since I was a young child, I really began to understand the word resting ruling and abiding in my life, after Pastor James' teaching and preaching.

    I had my first personal encounter with God and faith. I had a car issue for the first time with my 1997 Ford Escort. It was paid off so I had no car note. My grandfather had paid it off for my birthday one year so that I could free up some money. He also did it since he was the co-signer and had no idea what was going on in Atlanta. He felt better with it being paid off. I woke up in May of 2003 and said on faith, "I'm going to get me a new car today and it's going to be a PT Cruiser". Surely, God did what He said and I got me a PT Cruiser with faith and no money. I loved Jesus again for real He was showing up and showing out in my life. I never missed the money from Pin-Ups because he was just providing my every need, according to his riches and glory. Jesus began to tug at my spirit about Shawn. It was not until shortly after 2003, I shared that I had a daughter with some people in the congregation of Favor Baptist Church. I remember talking to Pastor Christian in the front of the church about my daughter, and he broke down the word responsibility. He told me, "If you respond to God, He will give you the ability to make it with your daughter in Atlanta. She is your responsibility." I got that word and prayed, then made provisions for my daughter to get back to Atlanta, GA with her mother. I was growing spiritually again with good word and a good church. I was coming into the knowledge of generational curses. My grandmother raised me, and I was basically falling into a generational curse of grandparents raising children. I decided to break the generational curse and raise my own child. By the time I got Shawn back with me, I could not discipline her without her calling and telling on me to her great grandmother and grandmother. She was a kindergartener and it was a struggle to deprogram and reprogram her. It got to the point that on some days I just wanted to give up on being a mother. I would say I want to send her back to my grandma. Being a mother is too much. She would hit me back if I tried to chastise her and my friends would tell me that I'm the parent. If she gets ten more whoopings, she's gone know that she can't hit her mother at 5 years old. I used to be late for work because she did not want her hair combed and we would play tug-of-war with the book bag. I would ask for it and she would refuse to give it to me. But as time grew on, she developed a liking to being with mommy and I had to learn how to love her again. I had to understand that I had not been in her life for a while on a full-time basis. I thought about how my mother and I's relationship was like that of sisters, because I was raised my entire life by my grandparents. I too used to tell on my mother to my grandparents. A generational curse was broken, by me taking my responsibility back while deprograming and reprogramming my daughter at 5 years old. Now she is 15 years old, I can't get her to go anywhere for a long period of time without wanting me. I encourage you as women that if you have children and are not raising them, go get your responsibility and fight the battle to break a generational curse. No longer will we accept people taking over our homes and invading our parental rights as mothers. Even though our parents mean well, we have to go back and take what the devil stole from us as mothers. He will use our kids to get our attention, if he can't get to us. Grandparents are wonderful and it takes a village to raise a child, but the mother is the most important person in the village. I took my responsibility and made sure she was first in my life. God put people in place to help me when I needed help. People need people and Jesus to get through life's events. He put people in place that I could trust and did not mind assisting me with Shawn. I wanted to continue going to school. Sometimes I had to go to work and drop her off to friends, until I got out of school. I sacrificed time and gas, sometimes driving from different sides of town, to make sure she was in a safe place with people I trusted. If I did not have a sitter, I took her right to school with me, and she would sit by the door of my classroom and do her homework. She has always been a very well-mannered child. That was a good thing for me as a mother, because people did not mind watching her for me. I continued to work and go to school regardless of life's ups and downs. Whatever the task we always made it through. I never had my lights turned off or was homeless. I always depended on myself and only called to my grandparents, if times were really hard. They rarely got that hard because Jesus was Jehovah Jirah, my provider.

At this time, my faith in the Lord was building fast. My friend and I, who I met at the Favor Baptist Church, made plans to go school shopping for our kids after Sunday service. How about by the time we got out of church and received the word, it was a change of plans. Pastor Christian preached about since you take care of God's house, God will build you a house. We got to the parking lot of Favor Baptist Church and all focus was on looking for houses. We went looking for houses, instead of school shopping for the kids. I was really getting to know Jesus in a more intimate way through his word; my faith was growing so big that I depended on him for everything. I had begun to experience some things in my life as a Christian, in this little church called Favor Baptist Church. I have seen miracles and actually had hands laid on me for the first time in my life, by Pastor Ruberts C. from Louisiana. He was a guest speaker at Favor Baptist Church, he prophesized into my life. "You will never worry again," is what he whispered into my ear, and the spirit took over me. I fell out, I was weak as could be on the church floor, and I was so slayed in the spirit that I could not get off the floor. I was crying. I only saw this on television and always wondered if it was real. I was amazed! I actually felt spiritually drugged up for about two weeks strong. From that experience with the Holy Spirit, I have never felt the same about Jesus and the Holy Spirit again. Since then, I have had hands laid on me, but never as strong as that powerful cleansing he performed. I have had so many experiences with the Lord at this point, and now I have a personal relationship with Pastor and Sister Christian as the foundation of my spiritual development. I thank them both for their love of God. I realized I was no longer growing up in the church but that the church was actually growing up in me. So after all I have experienced, surely if the man of God said I was going to get a house and it's supported by scripture, He's going to give me a house based on my faith. At this time, I had already been looking at a subdivision of townhomes. I had an old debt from 1997 at Southern University, which now decided to show up on my credit report in 2004 as a judgment. After I found that out I got discouraged about the house. But the husband of the dentist that I was working for at the time was a realtor. He said, "Let me have my people look at your credit. I'm sure they can get you into a home." I then decided I did not want to look for houses. I was not comfortable with my realtor being my boss's husband. I felt too much of my personal business was involved with work. I prayed about the process and I decided I did not need a realtor and then let my realtor go. I knew that my faith would not fail me as it related to God blessing me with a home. I have heard a word from the Lord through Pastor Christian as confirmation, regardless I'm standing on the word about getting into a home. I went back to the original subdivision and talked to the realtor on-site. She referred me to a friend at Bank of America mortgage loans. I went to fill out the pre-approval form and waited for the results. I never said anything about the judgment because I hadn't heard from the creditor and was not going to volunteer the information. When the realtor on-site called to schedule the appointment, the Lord told me to fast for three days. I was obedient to the Lord and did a three day fast. I went to meet the mortgage banker from the Bank of America location on Lavista Rd. in Tucker, Ga. I learned about fasting at Favor Baptist Church. We would do a "corporate fast" and "Daniel fast", and I began to grow and see manifestations from my sacrifice. Remember I never told the mortgage banker about the judgment. So when I arrived, she informed me that I was approved for a house and how much house I could afford. She informed me that I could get the townhome that I wanted. I even had enough to get a brand new townhome built from the ground up. I shouted in the office, in amazement of what God had done again and again in my life. I then asked her about my credit. I said, "It's something on my credit I was concerned about. I haven't said anything, but I wanted to know what you suggest, just in case it comes up." I explained that I had a judgment from Southern University from 1997 that I had never paid off. I then asked her what should I do about it. She said, "Well here on your credit report it's reporting: satisfied/never late". I was crying about what the Lord had done. I was like nobody but Jesus could have done that in such a perfect way. I just had seen a miracle done on my behalf again. No one can tell me what God can't and will not do for those that love him, and seek after His face. The prayers of the righteous avail much. I went through the process of a first time home buyers program. Later, I went to claim my lot on which my house would be built. I was so amazed by the process and Jesus was sure to get all the glory. By January 2005, God blessed me with the opportunity to become a home owner for the first time, a brand new townhome built just for me. Throughout the process I had to pay some bills off, so I was debt free and loving it. When I tell you I have never seen the righteous forsaken or his seed begging for bread. God has always provided my needs and I know what it means to have a ram in the bush. I was still going to school part-time, working and being a single mother. Life's events were still occurring but my faith has made me whole. Everything was going good for me in my opinion. I'm attractive, I work, I'm completing school, I love the Lord, and I'm a great mother.

But if you notice for a couple of years something was missing. I wanted to be loved by someone else, I wanted companionship. I could never say I had my own boyfriend or my own man. If you notice they were somebody else's. So I met a man, Mr. Right. He was tall, dark chocolate, bald headed and successful. Jesus knows how I feel about those chocolate dudes. We met and went out, and everything moved really fast. We began to do everything together. He was fun to be around and funny. He treated me like a queen and called me "babe." He was very affectionate. He gave me a nickname, Meek. Every time he called me that, it did something to me. He acknowledged me and introduced me as his girl, which made me feel very important compared to my past experiences. He took me on business trips and was proud that I was on his arm. We did everything together, so out of convenience, I stayed at his house majority of the time and even had my own key. It was all about me, Meek, his babe. I began to be intimate with him and battle with the Lord afterwards every time with conviction. I enjoyed it and then would repent. Repented flesh is always satisfied flesh. I never really told him that I was convicted, because I wanted my relationship so badly. So I was attracted to him, he talked good to me, treated me like a queen and yet we were fornicating. As the church folk would say, "straddling the fence". I was just all messed up in the mind. A friend of his had an all-white wedding which we were invited to. We complimented each other and always made the room light up when we were together. People always would give both of us compliments about each other. This day at the wedding, it was overwhelming and we had so much fun on the dance floor. After the wedding, we went home. I practically lived there so I would call it home. We were changing our clothes and he pulled me in the closet and pressed my back against the wall. He looked me into my eyes and said, "I love you and I don't want to ever be without you." That was the first time Mr. Right said "I love you" and from that day on it became an everyday occurrence. We would have talks about kids, marriage and even putting my townhome up for rent. We talked about being together forever daily and I felt like I was in love. Soon, I began to share with him about my relationship with God, and how I feel like I have fallen off on my church attendance. He said, "No problem babe. We will start going to church." We went to Favor Baptist Church a couple of times and he shared how he did not care for it. I actually was missing my church family, but wanted to keep my relationship with him. So we decided to try other churches, and by now I've visited so many churches I had lost count. I knew who was good or bad as it related to delivering the word. So we visited Beacon Baptist Church where Pastor McDonald resided. Pastor McDonald had just preached at Favor Baptist Church, and mentioned he was relocating from Macon, GA. I could not wait to hear the word. I felt that I was cheating on Pastor Christian and Sis Christian, but my flesh wanted my relationship. Pastor McDonald preached his socks off that day. My boyfriend's attention was focused on the word and when he started writing stuff down, I knew he liked it. Pastor McDonald said, "The only place you find 'success' before 'work' is in the dictionary." He liked that quote and wanted to go back to the church. We began to go to the church often and soon he led us to join together. We joined Beacon Baptist Church, and I felt like I had just left my best friend, Favor Baptist Church. I was in the car on the way home like OMG! What a Mistake! I did not pray about this. He is not my husband yet! What does this mean? Do I have two church homes: one for me and one for the both of us? Now I was confused and Satan is the author of confusion. Basically, I learned a great lesson. Never leave your church for a relationship that is not with your husband.

    Shawn was out of town for the summer, so they had never met. He knew that I had a daughter, and we discussed her and us. Again, I was thinking long term since we were joining a church together. He had a son and I had enjoyed spending time with his son, so I began to love him as well. I felt that since he was a father, he surely would accept my child. I also loved his fatherly insight and direction, as a good example, that he showed daily. He was raised in a two parent home, and from what I had seen, he had wonderful family values. He loved his mother more than I could put into words and I loved it too. I was so in love with being in love. We would go to the gym together, take showers together and ride bikes together. He loved the water so we would swim or go to the beach regularly. We would do spontaneous things, off the wall stuff, and laughed all the time. Like I said, he was fun to be around. One night, it was about to rain, and we were outside playing in the grass. We basically laid in the grass and waited for it to rain. As we kissed, the rain drops fell on us. We spoke sweet nothings to each other. Most of the time, it was not sexual. It was emotional, caring, sensitive actions that had my mind all messed up and crazy. I could not believe how in love I was with this person. I can say for the first time in my life, I was truly in love and never wanted the feeling to end. He also took good care of me and was very frugal about how he spent his money. Soon, my daughter came back to town and I introduced them. He brought her flowers and I felt that this was a good person to bring into her life. He asked her, "Do you want me to be your daddy?" I was shocked and interrupted with a gesture, like please not now. They would play outside with balls since she was a soccer player at the time and I would prepare meals. Sometimes he would help her with her homework and/or pick her up from school, if I needed assistance. Basically, he became an intimate part of me and Shawn's life. Soon he said he needed his space. That was the beginning of our relationship getting shaky. I began to feel insecure about our relationship. Gradually he began to separate himself from me. Now, I was trying to go to Jesus for help and understanding. Soon I gave my key back and started staying at my own house. All he ever told me was that he needed his space. My womanly intuition wanted to know what was going on. I noticed that he would not leave his phone around the house anymore. He started to keep it close by or in his case on his waist. I attempted to try to check his voicemails on his phone. I was thinking what could the passcode be either his last 4 digits of his social security number, his birthday or his son's birthday. I checked his voicemail for the first time. I decided to use his son's birthday. It was a success, and that was the first day. I started to listen to his voicemails. Of course, it was another woman or women. I could not tell who was important. They all left sweet, good messages. Of course, I never said anything. I played it off. One day, we were scheduled to go to church together, and usually I would stay at his house because he had an extra room for Shawn. He suggested I meet him in the morning. I was calling the whole night checking the voicemails. I would call anonymous, so that he would not answer. He never answered anonymous calls and would send them to voicemail, which is what I wanted. However, I still never knew who he was with, but of course, I knew it was another girl. The next day, Shawn and I met him at his house and we went to breakfast and to church. I could tell it was over without him saying anything. I could never understand why he did not just break up with me. Why did he keep saying he needs his space while still doing things with me? Of course, I knew more because of the voicemails. Every day, it bothered me to listen to them, and not say anything. I did not want to tell on myself and I did not want him to know that I invaded his privacy, because had I always trusted him in the past. Then I heard the hottest voicemail that stopped the press. The girl said, "I love you!" at the end. When I say seek and you shall find, knock and the door shall open, ask and you shall receive. I let the "cat out of the bag that day." Due to my emotions and feelings of being hurt, I told on myself and exposed the secret of checking his voicemails. I called the girl that left the message and Lord only knows what I said because I was hurt. By now, I find out that she was staying at his house and was officially his girlfriend. I was hurting, I had the strongest soul tie I could have ever thought possible. I was totally not in the picture at all, and it had only been three weeks since he officially called it quits and needed his space.

I had disappointed Jesus and myself with the decisions that I had made. I left my church to focus on this man, which appeared to be the man of my dreams and future husband. I always had written my daily thoughts in a journal as a sense of healing or release. I encourage most women to journal and keep most stuff between you and Jesus. Everything is understood so there's no need for a discussion. So just write it down, so you can prevent yourself from saying the wrong thing or having a lot of regrets. I took my thoughts and feelings right to Jesus. I went and purchased books. I bought Single Saved and Having Sex, and then I purchased the book Soul Ties. I read every book possible even the Bible. I could not eat, drink, and called into work almost three times a week. I was crushed and wanted answers because I was confused about our love. If you think about it, Jesus was probably like, "You are confused about your relationship with me." I started acting funny with Jesus when I got a boyfriend, and put him on the back burner. But this time, I put Jesus in the dugout for months as if I was embarrassed about our relationship. I became very depressed about life and hopeless. I cried every day and sometimes I would call and hang up in his face just to hear his voice. He wanted nothing to do with me because I had been checking his voicemails and now he had a new girlfriend. Then one day after I went through the motions and was trying to get it together, I decided to go to some group sessions and counseling for healing. I did not know where to start with my life. Of course, everything stopped and went lacking due to this sickness called a "soul tie." I finally completed two years at Atlanta Metropolitan College and transferred to Clayton State's healthcare management program. But I was not even attending school like I should. I eventually withdrew from school since I was so behind. School, work and everything went lacking. It was as if he was the only man in the world, or more important than Jesus. I used to pray to Jesus every day, "When will it go away?"

My story is to let any woman know to never invade a man's privacy and what you seek you will find. I know that I don't like for my privacy to be invaded. Also treat people like you want to be treated. I shouted to the top of my lungs, "Oh my God!" I made a mistake. Jesus please forgive me! I begged and pleaded with Jesus for forgiveness, mercy and most of all healing. Soon, I was healed feeling good about me and Jesus again. Now I'm at a different level in my walk and my friends have transitioned also. It's easy when you hang around people that think like you and have the same goals. Candace Crown, Mia Reid and I are not talking about strip clubs and sponsors any more. We are only talking about Jesus. I went back to Favor Baptist Church after the break-up. Favor Baptist Church and Joyce B. were having 6am prayer at their churches. One morning at prayer, I heard from Jesus to go to dental school. I prayed about timing and finances because I was a single mother.

Due to fear, I decided to go against what God said about dental school and I started to pursue completing my bachelor's degree in Health Care Management. I knew that with a bachelor's degree, I could have a career in dental sales or manage dental facilities. Then my friend, Elvern Shelton- Cooks, friends since Southern University, told me about this online school that would allow me to be at home with Shawn and finish my degree at the same time. I looked into it and submitted my transcripts. I went through the advisements and decided to go to school online. I went on to complete my degree at American Intercontinental University. I wanted to have a business administration degree with an emphasis in healthcare management. I related it to dentistry in order to approach going to dental school one day in the future when I got a release about the timing. I still never made the money I wanted to make, or lived the desired lifestyle I wanted for my family and I. Basically, my life consisted of mistakes that may appear to some as unstable in many ways. I view them as different learning seasons that I had to go through. Some of them were the turns that God used to get me back on track when I went astray. Minister White once said, "God's final decision is His original plan." So no matter how you go to the left, God has a way to pull you to the right and still have it work out for your good. I pushed on to complete school finally in 2007. I graduated with a bachelor's degree in Health care Management from American Intercontinental University. Since I was a non-traditional student, had changed schools and majors, I had more than enough credits combined. Like Maya Angelou said, "I wouldn't take anything for my journey." I'm proud of the good, bad and life mistakes that I have gone through. I know who I am and most importantly I know who's I am. My life is a living testimony to let the single mother that had a child out of wedlock know that if God did it for me, He sure can do it for you. Make Jesus the focus at all times, and be aware of the tactics of the enemy to get you distracted or off track. You are taught to teach and use what you have to express what's in your heart. This way you will be able to help others not to make the same mistakes. No one is exempt from mistakes, and in this life we will all make them. Remember God does not give you the spirit of condemnation or fear. We all have made mistakes and the truth be told, some of us still make them. The first name we call, if we know him as a savior, is JESUS!

Mica Callaway

Chapter 2
30 N Ticking

I was 29 years old and 30 thirty was approaching faster than I ever imagined. Of course, I felt like I should have had all my stuff together by the time I approach 30 years old. I'm still in school taking pre-requisites for dental school, trying to figure out when the educational season of my life will be complete. I'm looking back over my life at all the time I wasted. Thinking, if I hadn't got pregnant in college, I would be done with dental school by now. If I wouldn't have let that breakup tear me to pieces, I would be further along in my life by now. Looking at all the energy and time I wasted on a man that did not mean me any good. I'm about to be 30 and the clock is ticking! I want a husband and need somebody to help me. I've been doing this for a long time alone with no help. This was my thought process at almost 30-N Ticking.

In my world, by the time I turn 30, I should be married with a house, family and living happily ever after. I need to find out how to prepare for a husband. I need to know where to go, what to do and make it happen fast. I have always had a gift of gab, but why do I always have relationships that fail. This time when I get a boyfriend, I don't want a tall, dark and handsome one. That hurt me entirely too bad and that is my weakness. I loved him more than he loved me. This time I need a man that loves me more. So when we break up, it doesn't hurt as bad. I had created a list of what I wanted in my next mate. I hadn't even truly got over the break up that left a huge soul tie. Let me tell you ladies, men always find a way to keep it moving. Then it got better, I heard Mr. Right got married. What! How did he get married to somebody already? You sure it's not the girl after me? Nope. It's not the girl after you. I was still hurt and realized I still was not healed, and really could not believe the way that we broke up. I'm going to get me a husband and somebody that is in love with me. I'm telling God, "I deserve a husband, I got it going on. Who wouldn't want me as their wife?"

I met a guy in my biology course named Nick Haywood. He was smart and since I was coming back to school and interested in applying to dental school I needed all the help I could get and asked him to help me. He was quiet and did not talk much, but I knew I could get him to talk to me. He began to help me with my work, and attend study sessions that friends and I had. I was still seeing a guy friend in Chicago, IL, off and on; I flew back to Atlanta from a visit, the same day, a study session was about to occur. I did not have time to leave the airport and get my car. The study partner said, "I will send Nick the quiet guy to come and get you from the airport". Nick picked me up from the airport and we went to the study session, with an understanding that he would take me home when it was over. I never thought he was looking at me as attractive. I actually never looked at him, in any way, but to pass my class and gain his knowledge. I just looked at him as a cool guy. We had a study session at the study partner's house, and she was cooking shrimp and crab legs. The study partner said she needed something from the store. Nick volunteered to go, while we stayed at the house. When he left the study partner said "You know Nick like you?" I said, "Oh no! He is not my type, but he is very nice and he is a little cute in his own way." I appreciated him for picking me up from the airport, since we barely knew each other. So soon he returned and I began to check him out. He began to ask me questions about my trip, since he just picked me up from the airport. I shared how I was seeing a guy friend and that it was totally over. I made a mistake by going to Chicago. We laughed and carried on about our studies and the course. After the study session, he took me home. I explained to him, "I don't let men come to my home, but due to the circumstances, you will know where I live". He seemed very nice and polite, so I felt comfortable; after all we go to the same school. After that evening, every time we had class, he would ask me to go to dinner afterwards. I would go but realized he was spending a lot of money. I was not interested in him at the time; I just wanted to be his friend. So I felt it was no need to try to impress me, or wine and dine me because I was not interested. But he kept being real nice to me and I began to like it, and soon became attracted to his niceness. I was focused on Jesus and was still attending 6am prayer. By now, I'm going to every singles conference in the world. I'm back on track, and then Pastor T. C. came to Favor Baptist Church and preached. She said, "Ladies keep your legs closed." I had not had any sex and I wanted to please God in every way. The soul tie from Mr. Right was so serious. I was scared to have sex. I will admit we can always get a great word at Favor Baptist Church, which would convict you and transform your thinking. Then one day, Nick asked me out to a concert. He had two tickets. I accepted his invite. I was single and trying to occupy my mind and it was time to move on from my ex-boyfriend. We talked that night and really enjoyed ourselves. He got to know a little about me and I got to know a little about him. After the concert it was late. He invited me to stay at his house. He insisted that I sleep in his bed, but I refused. I did not want any spirits he was connected to. I happily slept on the couch. We began to spend a lot of time with each other and since he lived with his sister. When he came over to my house to study, I could not get him to go home. I could not figure out why he never wanted to go home. So I began to let him stay, and one day he had an argument with his sister in front of me. I admit I was a bit confused because he was so nice. I never ever heard him curse until that day. He called his sister a B***H. I felt like he just disrespected my house. Now my home is all anointed at this time. Favor Baptist Church had every member bringing their own oil to church, so it could be anointed. My whole house was cleansed of spirits and soul ties, and cursing was elementary, so we never had that issue.

We had a real talk that day as friends. I realized he had no clue about the Bible. He told me that his grandfather was a preacher. I was still like where is the Jesus in him. I asked if he was a Christian, he said, "Yes". But a lot of stuff did not make sense. I started to lift him up in prayer. He told me that he did not have a Bible of his own. He started to go to church with me more and I was trying to be an example. I explained about no sex prior to marriage and showed him scripture. Later, I fell to temptation and we were intimate. The next day Jesus gave me a beating in the spirit. I was convicted and cried out to Jesus once again. I violated my temple and felt Jesus was disappointed in me. I prayed for forgiveness and was greatly appreciative of the fact that Jesus does not give us the spirit of condemnation. I tried to explain to him what happened and showed him scripture, but I was not successful with explaining. I noticed that explaining conviction, condemnation, and fornication were like noise instead of a spiritual deposit to him. I contacted a spiritual friend from church for assistance. She invited us to her house to discuss the Bible, and explain what occurred in my spirit after fornication. I was praying he would understand and step up to the plate spiritually as a man. Fall semester was about to end. We were inseparable at this time. I began to like him. He was always so nice and attentive to me, and I was not even concerned about the stuff that used to matter to me. I accepted him as he was.

All my friends and family began to like him as well. I really was not thinking about a husband like I had been prior to 6am prayer. I was focused on Jesus and being his friend. As you all know, prayer changes things and if you go through enough, your desire for God to make you whole will happen. After a while, we became very comfortable with each other, and brought the New Year in at Watch Night Service at Favor Baptist Church. And all I know is he wanted to make me happy and be with me all the time. He said, "I'm a quick learner and I will catch up with you soon spiritually". I began to really like him, but I internally battled with his salvation and his personal relationship with God. I knew where I needed my mate to be spiritually, as the head of my life and he was not even close to being that. I prayed about it and decided to part ways, even though it was not easy. I still wanted to be his friend and never liked hurting his feelings, because he was so into me and was so nice. I used to wonder what he is going to do if I leave him. He was so attached in such a short period of time. We finally broke up and after church I planned to take some small items he left at my house to him. I went to church that morning and for the first time he was not with me. He was good for attending church, but it was something about his heart. I never felt he was sensitive to the Holy Spirit. I was still confused about his salvation. He explained he was saved and gave his life to Christ, but had never been baptized. Again, I still accepted him for him and showed the love of Christ at all times, not judging, but taking it to the Lord in prayer. I arrived at his house to give him his things and he asked to talk to me. He sat across from me and I could tell in his eyes, he was hurt about the separation. I don't fully remember the conversation, all I remember, is he said, "You are the best thing that has ever happened to me". My heart melted. I tried to explain to him that we are different and you need to be with somebody that thinks like you. I was trying to speak in terms that were on his level and avoid using spiritual terms. He never understood being "unequally yoked", so I avoided spiritual conversation. Finally, after we talked he persuaded me to give him a chance and more time and that he desired to be the man I needed him to be for my life. So we continued to be friends. We did not have a title for one another. We were just friends that were together all the time. We did things for each other, but I never thought of it as a relationship. We were officially just hanging out. But at my age, hanging out can be a mistake, depending on where you are in your life. At 30-N Ticking a woman should be dating with a purpose, not hanging out, and a saved woman especially does not need to be engaging in pre-marital sex. So the boundaries where established in our relationship and we did not entertain fornication, to avoid me feeling convicted. He began to stay at my house often and one day he started to discuss marriage. He would wake up in the morning and say, "Let's go get married!" I desired to have a marriage with pre-marital counseling session, long engagement and a wedding; and I was informing him of what I wanted and desired every time the conversation occurred. Time went by and soon he officially asked me to marry him, and we began pre-marital counseling at the church. We would complete our homework sessions and everything was fine, but it was some things that just did not make sense or sit right in my spirit, but I continued the relationship.

We would converse about the bible and spirituality, and since he was new in Christ, some stuff I wanted him to get fast; and really expected for him to know already. After all, your grandfather is a preacher, is all I'm thinking in my head. Soon, everything began to move fast with planning a wedding, and decisions we made were not really what I wanted they were what his parents wanted. But I'm thinking everything will be okay, Jesus is able. He would give me his parent's Mr. and Mrs. Haywood's opinion about how they did not have a wedding. Suggesting that we don't have a wedding because they didn't have one and I was totally against it. Everything we planned they compared to what they did. I'm thinking to myself, well that is what they did, and my family had many weddings in the past before too. Mr. and Mrs. Haywood were cool, but I was focused on my relationship with Nick and not them. My thought process then was "I'm not marrying them", and we never saw them much anyway. Of course, the Bible talks about cleaving to your spouse: "Therefore a man shall leave his father and mother and be joined to his wife, and they shall become one flesh"

(Genesis 2:24). I'm sure he will do that when we get married. With everything moving fast and no definite date in my mind, we soon stopped attending the pre-marital counseling sessions. We battled all the time about what his parents wanted and not what I wanted. I had parental advice and parental opinions from my grandparents, but I have been grown and on my own; of course, I make my own decisions. So his parents never had a wedding and his mom's first ring came from the pawn shop, until they could upgrade to another ring. My grandmother had over 4 wedding sets and had been married for over 60 years and advised me it doesn't matter about the ring. What matters is his heart. The ring was a small issue and I never shared with him those discussions with my parents.

All I know is my grandfather said, "It's the man's responsibility to get you a ring and I'm concerned about your spiritual compatibility." My grandfather and I were very close and he never met the soon to be in-laws. But I would share conversations about them with him.

As the time approached for my grandpa to come to Atlanta and meet the family I was about to marry, he decided not to give me his blessing on getting married. He did not want to give me away or walk me down the aisle. He informed me he had no desire to meet the soon to be in laws and would not financially help me with the wedding as he promised. He stated, "I changed my mind, but I will always be here if you need me regardless of the decisions you make. You are still my child, you can always come home." He never told me why he made such a decision, and at the time, I wished I was in Kansas City to talk to him. So without discussing this with Nick I scheduled a trip for us all to go and visit my family. My grandfather and I's relationship was so close that I never wanted to disappoint him. At the time, I did not understand because he had always given me what I desired. The first thing I thought about when the marriage discussion began was my grandfather giving me away. Since he was over 70 years old, I better hurry up so he can give me away. A fairy tale dream I had since a little girl. My fiancée and I flew to Kansas City. He had not really seen a lot of snow in his life time, and as we approached the Kansas City airport, he looks out the small window pane in amazement of the snow. I will never forget when we went outside and made a snowman, and played in the snow. I never told my fiancée about the conversation with my grandpa; because I know regardless of what, my family does not judge and will always love everybody. The trip was nice, my grandfather and my fiancée, had conversations amongst themselves that I'm sure went well; because he was a great guy that everybody loved. But the private conversation daddy and I had amongst us, went a little like this, "I don't know nothing about Georgia, and in case of an emergency, it's too far for me to travel at my age. And I don't ride airplanes! I am concerned and know a lot about life, and marriage is not an easy road".

"The concern that I have is the fact that you love church and God, I know that because I know you. How are you going to marry somebody, that father said to your face, "I don't like church?" He said, "See when you call me and share stuff with me about that family, you are about to marry into, I feel like something isn't right. Then one day you called and told me that Nicks father said, 'I don't like church'. My grandfather said there it is, that's a problem". He said, "Just keep on living and people will show you them. All you know is, that you are about to be 30, its time to get married in Mica's world. But the question is, 'Is it Gods time for you to get married?' And is this God's mate for you?" I replied, "Daddy, I know, but I believe God is taking care of that. He goes to church with me and we have started to pray, and he is getting better with his knowledge about Christ". He said, "Awe okay, I'm sure you got all the answers. I wish you the best but you don't have my blessing". We continued our trip and I never said a word to my fiancée. As we prepared to head back to Atlanta, my grandfather of course, gave us both individually some money to put in our pockets. That's his way of saying I love you. I went to the Lord and prayed, "Lord I know that you can do exceedingly above all that I can ever ask or think.

Please save my fiancé and allow him to be the man that God has called him to be". I went to tell my grandpa goodbye, then I said, "Daddy we gone be all right, watch and see, God is going to save him". He replied, in his sarcastic voice and a smile on his face, "Oh I see".

Now, it's about 6 months after we met at the study group. Boy how time has flown by. We are always together, and he is always nice to Shawn and I. He has met my family and I have met his. We placed a wedding ring in layaway to avoid accruing any debt. In the meantime, his mother kindly let me wear her first wedding set. He is still at my house all the time and Lord knows I don't want to fornicate. He has told me he loves me, so we decided to get married for my 30th birthday. All because of 30-N Ticking the week of my 30th birthday, I got married. I completed my bachelor's degree finally. I got it all together real fast in Mica's world on Mica's timing.

To all my single, saved women reading this, I'm sure you can relate to having this feeling at some point in your life. But it has happens to most women as their time clock is ticking. They may not be woman enough to tell you, but this book is my release of my past faults, and I'm going to be real and tell my mistakes related to the marriage:
- We were not equally yoked
- We did not complete marriage counseling
- I did not have my parents blessing (which in my opinion is a mistake)
- He did not have any knowledge of Jesus Christ
- He did not propose with a ring

The scripture that comes to mind, when I think of this chapter is: "But if they cannot exercise self-control, let them marry. For it is better to marry than to burn with passion." (1 Corinthians 7:9). You always want a man that leads you closer to Christ, than to himself, regardless of passion. You shall desire to have self- control and practice patience with abstinence. If you do that you will not have to scream, "OMG! WHAT A MISTAKE!"

Chapter 3
I'ma Save Him

After six fantasy months of dating, I'm married now. For those six months, he was everything I needed him to be except, I battled with confidently knowing if my husband was truly saved. According to him he did not have a church home, he did not own a Bible, he had never been baptized, but he was saved. The only person that knows about people's salvation is Jesus, if they are not leading by example. I was not judging him and I never felt like his heart was there spiritually. When it came to family matters, let me say I saw the signs, but ignored them because I felt I did not marry the family but him. When we met, I was focused on the fact that "Your grandfather is a preacher". You should know everything about Jesus, spirituality and religion. I began to analyze a situation that should have only been lifted up in prayer prior to marriage. After all, it's not our grandparent's relationship with Christ that saves us. As my husband, I wanted instant results as it related to his knowledge and relationship with Christ. I knew how I wanted him to be and how I wanted him to talk as my husband.

Ladies we all have had a relationship, that we really wanted to work with a man, which did not demonstrate the qualities of a saved man. I'm guilty of seeing a Godly man praise the Lord and preach, and then want that type of man for myself. However, we never know what that type of man is doing outside of the church. We want what we see without the unknown. We all know that what looks good is not always good. We seldom look at the men in the congregation, that are not working in ministry, as if they are not as saved as the man preaching or working in the ministry. We often will still date men that don't attend church or own a Bible, until he is in a relationship with us. After a couple of months of dating, we expect him to jump on the band wagon. We expect instant results since he is dating us, we want him to be saved, sanctified and filled with the Holy Ghost. When we met him he was not in church, remember you met him at the _____ (you can fill in the blank). I used to assume that all men should already know how to pray, and that church attendance and spiritual growth is important.

The marriage began to move very fast. We married in March. Shortly after we had joint everything, even checking accounts. We purchased a home together in August and decided to be landlords. We rented my first home out as rental property. Since he was the man, we agreed for him to handle everything related to renters and showing property. I signed papers for him to be power of attorney over my property.

As time went on, I thought he was sweet and had great qualities as a man, but not as a Godly man. I desired to have a Godly man and understand that people can be at different places in their Christian walk. I thought about the qualities he had as a man that made me marry him. The one that stood out was he loved me beyond compare and was a good provider. He loved me more than Jesus Christ who died for him. I began to ask Jesus why he loves me more than you. I never heard an answer from Jesus and through impatience, I decided I'ma save him. Yep...I 'ma save him! Not JESUS! ME! You already know I'm on my way to another mistake!

I purchased his first Bible foe him. It was a blue NIV study Bible with his name engraved on the front in silver cursive letters, and name tabs of the books of the Bible, on the side for easy access. He actually would read it in his spare time because he was a reader. I noticed he would read it more when we had disagreements, and was quick to talk about the stories, when he was on my bad side to impress me. He began to learn some things that were shocking to him. Such as, he did not know, that you can file your tithes and offering on your taxes at the end of the year. He never knew that the church sends yearly contribution statements. He celebrated Christmas his entire life so I could never find the connection. I began to tell him what to do like he was in salvation church school. Now that you are the head of my life you need to pray and take your family to church etc. He was not doing that before he met me, so why would he start now? Again, we expect a man to already know that this is an important part of raising a family. Most of the time, if those values and morals were not instilled in the man as a child growing up, he has no clue what you are talking about.

Like I said, I battled with confidently knowing if my husband was saved, so I started at the beginning. I remember as a little girl we started to learn the romans road to salvation first: Romans 3:23, Romans 6:23 Romans 5:8 and Romans 10:9. As kids, we knew all you have to do is believe in your heart that Jesus died for our sins, and rose on the third day to be saved. He soon said he believed that statement. I'm relieved that he is saved! As I wiped sweat from my head, Yes! He believes Jesus died for us and rose on the third day. Yippee! What a load lifted ~Waiting to Exhale~. He was basically doing what I required, but not what was in his heart or required of the Lord. Christianity is a heart thing!

I found a little quiet space in the home, it was my prayer closet, and I made sure the house was anointed. He was my husband and I wanted him saved, and filled with the Holy Spirit. After we said, "I DO", of course we became a target for the enemy to destroy. Two weeks after marriage, I saw another person in my husband. He began to curse in the home, and now the closet smoker is exposed. Oh my God! I 'ma save him.

The devil does not like marriage or unity. As the head of our home, the devil will start at the top with husbands and work his way down, all the way to the children if you allow it. I was standing on the word: "A wise woman builds her house, but with her own hands a foolish one tears hers down." (Prov. 14:1) I began to build my house and made sure that I spoke kind words to my spouse. I made sure that I spoke kind words about him as well. A woman should never share her household business with the world, friends or family. So I never told anyone the change that took place after I said "I DO!" I began to participate in every wife challenge available such as:

30-Day Husband encouragement challenge (Our Life his way)

The 30-Day Spouse encouragement challenge (Science of Marriage Blog)

The 30-week husband encouragement challenge (A Clean Heart. Com)

30-Day wife encouragement challenge (Strength for today)

Diary of a stay at home mom challenge. I was not even a stay at home mom but we needed help

30-Day husband challenge encouragement group (cafe mom)

As you can see, his salvation became a full time job. Now why do I have to explain to a grown man that you do not curse at your wife? Ummm, because he is not saved. I began to need help explaining to him his role in a marriage and as the head of our home. Soon, I began to feel sick. He would say," Ain't nothing wrong with you" even though I told him I was in pain. He wouldn't let me go to the doctor unless I had a certain amount of money saved in the bank, since I did not have insurance at the time. The pain got so bad that I called my mom and told her. She said, "Go to the doctor and I will pay for the bill". That same day Nick and I took off from work to go to the doctor. He also agreed to go to see a counselor. I found out I was pregnant that day. While I was pregnant, if I just wanted to get a break from the drama, I would check into a hotel for a day to rest and have a peace of mind. We agreed to attend counseling sessions. We met with a variety of counselors due to different request on both of our parts.

We attended all of them for different reasons at different times. Let me explain. I wanted a Christian counselor with the foundation to be the word of God. Amongst the counselors, they were all great Christian based programs with different perks that they individually brought to the table. I perceived our situation and stories were so deep compared to the average couple that we needed someone with certain licenses or letters behind their name. Some counselors were great friends, pastors, and single, divorced and/or had LPC (Licensed Professional Counselor), M Ed (Masters of Education) CTRT (Certified Trauma Resolutions Therapy), LCSW (Licensed Clinical Social Worker) certificate and other credentials. We soon narrowed the search down and agreed we wanted someone that was married with kids, and had certain credentials related to LPC, M Ed, CTRT. We wanted this because of the results that we got such as performing a personality assessment to review the personalities we were trying to bring together. We landed a great counselor at Trinity Counseling Center, LPC M Ed, and CTRT. We didn't mind the hour drive to get there after work and the Atlanta traffic. The more things that were revealed about both of us in counseling caused the drama to be raised higher and higher. Remember now, we did not complete marriage counseling and dated for only 6 months. I began to get upset not only with my husband, but with myself and the decision that I had made to think I can save him.

It began to be entirely too much work to try to convince a grown man that: "Husbands, love your wives, just as Christ also loved the church and gave himself for her" (Ephesians 5: 25). I use to say, "I can't wait for him to be saved, so he will love me as Christ loved the church in the Bible". I began to seek fasting options on the internet at:

Fasting for breakthrough (Covenant Partner marriage

restoration)

Fast for your marriage (Beautiful Womanhood)

Prayer and fasting for marriage (Breakthrough church)

Spiritually unequal marriage (Breakthrough living)

The more I prayed, fasted and joined a challenge, the harder it got in my home and marriage. The more I loved and the more I demonstrated love, the meaner he got and the madder I got. He continued to curse in the home, even around the kids, as if it was normal conversation with no remorse or apologies. If I was at a private counseling session, he would think I was doing something bad or against our marriage. As the journey got harder, the nice person that I dated for 6 months became someone I did not even know.

The verbal abuse was so bad. He talked to me like I was a stranger or a dog on the street. I had never felt so disrespected in my life as a daughter, woman or mother. I did not want this vocabulary in my home for Shawn to hear. As it was totally against, anything I had ever exposed her to in her entire life. He began to curse so bad, that I would say, "If you feel the urge to curse just keep it to yourself or try broadening your vocabulary". My own husband was mocking me when I prayed and telling me, "God isn't gone help you." I used to imagine myself hitting him as hard as I could when he would degrade me with his words. After a while, I would just leave the house to save myself from getting physical. I had to leave the home environment, and sometimes just get away to a healthy, peaceful place, just to get my thoughts together. I just wanted something I thought was very simple, to get along with my husband and be happily married. During one of our counseling sessions, he expressed how curse words were okay in his opinion. He stated, "I was raised in a home, where my parents cursed at me as a child and around me all the time, and I turned out just perfectly fine." Even though, we are spending countless dollars on counseling he was always angry and I didn't know why.

I believed God for my marriage and my husband to be saved. I was leading by example and wanted him to see my light shine. God revealed to me how we were unequally yoked. But we got married based on our timing and not Gods timing. I had to work harder than God ever intended for me to work because it was a marriage that was not called by God. This is what happens when you do things out of God's order, a lesson I was learning the hard way. Soon, I realized I'm tired of trying to save him and the devil was wearing me out in my home. I was like a tire in the mud, just going around and around, but never going anywhere and never getting any results. Now I was not happy with myself and my walk as a Christian. I began to feel uncomfortable working in ministry and at home living with an angry person. My husband was not supportive about anything that I did in church. I wondered if I was a vessel that God could still use. I began to question who I was and who's I was. I would ask, "Why me Lord? Why me?" I realized the verbal abuse was affecting my self-esteem as a woman and mother. My husband did not understand how I felt because he did not want to understand.

We were going through a lot in the early days of marriage. I would try to call Mr. and Mrs. Haywood for assistance and support regarding the verbal abuse around me and the kids. They just always made up excuses for Nick, as if it was okay for me to be mistreated as a wife, or our children to be exposed to such behavior. Then one day while we were visiting Mr. and Mrs. Haywood, Mr. Haywood called Mrs. Haywood a b***h and laughed. She looked embarrassed with a facial expression as if she wanted to say, "Don't embarrass me in front of them." That day God gave me a revelation of how Nick was raised. The expectations I had for my husband to bring his family to a place of peace, or for my mother –in- law to correct her son, would most likely never happen. It would cause them to go against their family beliefs and how they raise their children. Like he stated to the counselors, "I was raised in a home where my parents cursed at me as a child, and around me all the time and I turned out just perfectly fine."

Final Remarks:

Ladies, we don't want to come off as judgmental, but we really want to lead people closer to Christ by accepting them as they are. Jesus accepted us as we were. My goal is to lead people closer to Christ as a living example. I never wanted to lose my witness or be looked at as a hypocrite. Our families and loved ones can't save us from ourselves or our decisions.

God has the last say and God is going to do heart surgery on Nick. He will be saved and be a mighty man of God one day. Even though I use to think he was crazy, God told me to stop putting my mouth on him because he is the father of my child. Don't call him out of his name. Your words have power. The devil will use anybody and I'm guilty of the devil using me. I used to blame it on other people and the Lord said to me, "You are ruled by nothing but the word of God. God will not accept an excuse from you anymore. Grow up." God holds us accountable for our own actions. Of course, we don't have the power or the patience to save any man.

Chapter 4
DRAMA 911

It's usually a tragedy that occurs or a pivotal moment in life, which brings you into the loving arms of Jesus. That is if you know him as a savior like I do. The tragedy will push you into praise and worship. You begin to experience a joy that surpasses all understanding. A peace of mind that is priceless and a personal intimate experience with the spirit is all that you need. I finally experienced an intimate relationship with the Lord through my pain, hurt and confusion. I'm healed from people bondage so I could care less what people think. This is my time to praise God and accept his presence in my life. Now when I see people praising God in different ways, I don't have to know their story to understand their glory after an experience.

All of these elements led up to my discussion of The Root Cause, Marriage Drama, and Family Drama that lead to the moment of "I Hate Being Married":

The Root Cause:
I had never experienced so much drama in my life until I got married. It was a total 180 degree turn from what I expected or wanted. We all as women have a fairy tale dream of how our life

will be when we get married. We expect it to just come together like coloring inside of the lines and connecting the dots. We assume that everything is going to be perfect. Well what a rude awakening I had for my first marriage. I did not know who I married. I thought he was the devil for a long time. I guess he was a wolf in sheep's clothing. They can only be somebody else for a little while. We married in March and purchased our first home together by August. I would come home from work and he would start arguing with me about stuff that did not make any sense. You know the kind of arguments that seem made up because the other person just wants to fight or argue. He would bring up my ex-boyfriends and relationships, which I had not thought anything about. I was curious about where this was coming from, since we were fine and never had these issues prior to marriage. He started bringing up things about my past and calling me a liar, and I never knew what he was talking about. I felt like I was the most honest person I knew. I tell the truth even if it makes me look bad. I was healed from my past mistakes and now I'm ready to live a saved married life with my husband, and live happily ever after. I shared everything and anything under the sun with him during the six months that we dated. But my life did not predict my future or how I felt about my husband. I married him for him and nothing else. I did not care about materialistic stuff or money. I was confident that I could accomplish anything that I put my mind to, and being a survivor was already in my vocabulary. During our marriage, I noticed that I kept having problems with my email address and password. Every time I would try to check my emails, my password did not work. I started writing my passwords down and making sure that I kept them private. I changed security password questions and was soon aware that someone was going into my emails, so I changed every security question with an answer that was not true.

One day, he was furious when he came home and the biggest argument occurred. He started saying stuff again that did not make sense. Soon he told on himself that he had been going into my email accounts, and reading all of my sent emails as far back as 2005. That was two years prior to me meeting him. Now it is almost 2008 and I barely remember what happened last month, let alone 2-3 years ago. It was not that I was lying about past relationships, but I really felt like it was my past and truthfully some of it I had forgotten, unless you told me what you were talking about. I personally felt like I should not have to talk about my past relationships with my husband. After all we are married now and checking my emails against my consent is a violation of my privacy. I feel that when you start dating a new person, you should not have to spend much time talking about the people prior to your relationship as it is so insignificant. I was thinking that Nick was tripping to bring unnecessary drama into our current marriage and home.

Now I understood why he would come home angry because he was reading emails. I never cheated on him or did anything to violate my marriage, and there was nothing currently available for him to be upset with his wife about. I was thinking, after all I'm your wife and the past is the past. He started telling me that I never loved him and that was not true. I tried to do everything I could to explain and express my love for him. But he never did the same in return. It was give, give, give and take, take, take. I needed to feel loved and trusted as a wife since I never violated my marriage. Soon, he felt that I could not have male friends and all my female friends had to be married. He felt that a married woman has no business with single women. But most of my friends where still single and I felt that they were my friends prior to marriage. I asked why I had to lose my friends because I had gotten married. He had female friends that were his friends prior to the marriage. They would even come over to our house to visit, and later I found out that him and one of his female friends had been intimate in the past. But since I'm not insecure, I did not mind that they were still friends and I even allowed him to get massages from her since she was a massage therapist. He began to have rules in the home and treat me as if I was a child.

RULES:
You cannot go anywhere unless you take the kids. Not even 6am prayer.
Married women have no business being out of the house after 9pm.
I couldn't listen to gospel music while driving with him in the car.
I could not get my hair and nails done like I used to prior to marriage. He felt that it was a waste of money.
I could not buy what I wanted to buy even though I worked a job.
I could not go where I wanted to go with whom I wanted to go with.
I could not make my own decisions about my career and goals. He was not supportive about me going to dental school anymore and felt that two people could not go to school at the same time, even though when I met him we were both attending school.
The same thing that I did in my past is now happening in my marriage. That must be karma. He never explained, apologized or felt any remorse for checking my old sent emails. The root cause to DRAMA 911 was TRUST & INSECURITY.

MARRIAGE DRAMA:
Every now and then we would attend a counseling session by everyone that was considered to be the best, or who was available since we needed prompt attention. I always wanted to get along but it was never possible. I began to miss my family and wanted to go home to see my grandparents and be around people that loved me more. So I booked a flight and prepared to go visit my family alone. Nick did not agree with a wife going on trips alone, even if it was to see her family. But he could do whatever he wanted to do, because I treated him like a grown man and not a child. I also did not have trust issues. As I was preparing to leave town, he decided to take every suitcase in the house to work with him. I could not

find a suitcase to pack my clothes. I asked a friend to use her luggage and as I drove down Camp Creek Parkway to her house, I saw Nick driving in the opposite direction. He had a car full of suitcases piled up in the vehicle. I just continued on to my friend's house, got her suitcases and returned home to pack my things. When I arrived at the airport to check in with AirTran, they said that I did not have a flight to go anywhere listed in their system. I gave them my confirmation number and they looked up my reservation and explained that the reservation had been canceled. I explained in anger that I did not cancel my flight and my plane was about to leave. So I tried to use my phone to look up my flight information on my email. I could not access my email account, and at that time I realized, Nick had hacked into my email account again and canceled my flight. Since I paid with my credit card, there was still a credit on my account with AirTran. I immediately rebooked my flight and made the plane to go see my family on time. I was furious as I ran through Hartsfield International Airport. Words could not explain how I felt about Nick cancelling my flight. I arrived in Kansas City and proceeded to get a rental car to surprise my family. My credit card kept saying declined. I knew that we had money in the account and that there was more than enough since we had just gotten a nice tax return also. I called the bank to check my account and the account balance said: "NEGATIVE ONE THOUSAND ONE HUNDRED AND FIFTY SEVEN DOLLARS". I checked the history, it said: "WITHDRAWAL EIGHT HUNDRED DOLLARS, WITHDRAWAL EIGHT HUNDRED DOLLARS, WITHDRAWAL EIGHT HUNDRED DOLLARS, ETC". I hollered to the top of my lungs, "WHAT! Forgive me Jesus." I called Nick angry and in rage, "WHAT DID YOU DO WITH THE MONEY IN THE BANK?" He said, "I'm sorry. I made a mistake. I did not want you to leave me and I did not know what to do. I withdrew all the money out of the bank, not thinking about the checks that have not posted. I made a mistake, I'm about to call the bank now and get it straight." I said, "Where is all of our money?" He said, "It's at home."

You have got to be cautious of people that will hurt themselves to hurt you. I don't care how mad I am with my spouse. I would have never put Nick in a predicament, where he could not eat or have a dime in his pocket. I did not have much cash on me at the time. So I contacted my grandfather and he came to the airport to pick me up, and we had a long talk as I drove home to see my grandma. I was crying and talking to my grandpa about the money. My grandfather said, "I don't want to hear nothing else! I don't understand what type of man he is or what type of man raised him. A real man will never leave a woman and her kids in a predicament where they cannot eat or survive. He is dangerous! When you said his own father doesn't like church, I knew that is where the problem lies, his father." I stayed home in Kansas City for a while, but of course, I had to return to the drama in Atlanta due to work and Shawn's school.

The cursing and treating me bad made me not want to be intimate with him anymore. But most of all, not being a concerned husband when I was sick. He would holler at me saying, "You need to spread those legs! Yo m****f*****g as*, I call it like I see it b***h!" I got tired of the fighting, cursing, arguing and trying to be controlled, but he never got sick and tired of it. I began to have sex with him just to keep the peace.

The marriage was like peaks and valleys. One minute we were cool, the next we were enemies. When it was good it was good, but when it was bad it was very, very bad. So bad, that by this time in the marriage, I attempted to get a divorce twice and after the second divorce consultation, I realized I needed a plan. During the consultation the attorney advised me to wait until the baby was born, since I was pregnant with his first son. The attorney explained the details and reasoning behind it. He explained that bringing a child into the divorce would change the dynamics. It was not like a break up and two people could just go their separate ways. We were still attending counseling from time to time. But the counselors never understood that he was still treating me bad, when we got home. He was very good at trying to persuade people into believing that he was the victim. But people that actually were witnesses knew that if it was that bad, he would have left by now. By now, I see that Mr. and Mrs. Haywood are not going to rescue me and my children or offer any assistance to help us towards a peaceful marriage. I began to feel that they wanted him to mistreat me and my children. My family was in Kansas City and they decided that they did not want to be involved, since it was a marriage that they did not bless. They would still always send me their prayers. Through counseling sessions he had explained that, "He had to hurry up and marry me or he was going to lose me." Later he explained that he got me pregnant on purpose. I loved both of my children and knew that the marriage was not a healthy environment to bring children into. I also knew that having a baby would place my plans to attend dental school on the back burner.

The drama continued, he would bring up my past and say things that were really hurtful, that I was healed, saved and set free from prior to meeting him. He would talk bad about my family for no reason. At this time, I began to allow the Devil to use me also. I was not a curser when I met him. But now I'm cursing, mad and in rage. I'm demonstrating the behavior he had been demonstrating since we got married. Afterwards, I would feel convicted and apologize to him and God because I knew that it was wrong. I immediately began to fast and pray harder, due to my behavior and losing my witness. After a while, it was routine to curse, fight and ask for forgiveness. I knew the behavior was stupid and immature but he never wanted peace. It was like he looked for drama all the time and was never happy with me.

Soon, a couple of friends moved to Atlanta from my hometown. I was excited to have my close friend from middle school, who is also close to the family. They all decided to come over to my house with their spouses and kids. Nick decided to put some meat on the grill and we all were going to the movies. I was praying that he would act normal and not embarrass me in front of my friends. My friends and I went to get the movie tickets early, and were chilling at the house until it was time to go. When it was time to go to the movies, Nick decided he did not want to go and was upset that I did not fix his plate when we ate because I was attending to our infant. So I was still going to the movies since after all, I had already paid for the tickets and never get to go anywhere with friends. I told Nick, "Okay, you don't have to go with us." My friends decided to drive their own cars, so that when the movie was over they could go straight home. As I backed out of the driveway, with the kids in the car, Nick runs out to the car and busts my tires with a Phillips screw driver in front of my friends. He runs back into the house and my friends get out of their cars shocked. "What is going on with him?" they asked. I responded, "Can I ride with y'all to the movies?" My friend since middle school said, "Sure." I was so calm she could not believe it. As we drove to the movies I called Nick and said, "When you finish with your temper tantrum you can come to the movies. I have your ticket." He said, "I'm not going. I'm staying home." I said, "Okay" and enjoyed my movie. I went home that night and I had both of my kids with me at the movies. We were already in separate rooms at the time, so I went to bed. The next morning I woke up and got ready to go to church. He was outside fixing my tire to my car, so I asked him if I could use his car to go to church. I went to church and praised God like never before. I say this to say, I stopped reacting to everything that he did to me. I stopped losing my witness and tried to lead by example. I ignored drama and begged God for peace of mind in the midst of what I was going home to everyday. I was focused on Jesus and not the issue. I still never knew why he was and remained to be so mean to me for no reason.

 Saturday, November 17th was the first day that we had a physical encounter. It was a verbal altercation that lead to a physical altercation, due to him cursing and calling me a B***H. I was big about no cursing in my house prior to marriage especially towards me. I feel strongly that cursing is ignorant and very disrespectful. For the kids to see my husband and their father, cursing like an ignorant disrespectful man in his home was unacceptable. I will never forget the day, because it was the first time he called me a B***H in my face. I was so shocked and devastated. I almost lost my breath. I hollered to the top of my lungs "I'm your wife! I'm your wife! I'm going to call your mother and tell on you." Thinking that as a woman she would be on my side. He said my momma feels like "If you act like a B*T*H, you get called a B*T*H" as he looked at me like I was the enemy and not his wife. My instant reaction was to swing on him. I then swung at him, but I missed and he pulled me over his leg and held me down on the bed. He gave me 5 hard swats with his hand on my butt, as if I was his child. As I rose up, the closest thing to me was a lamp on the side of the bed. I hit him as hard as I could with the lamp and busted his head. I really did not mean to hurt him, but it was my immediate reaction. I saw blood and he was hollering, "You hit me!", as if he did not do the same to me. I ran into Shawn's room scared, because I knew he was about to beat the living day lights out of me. I ran into my Shawn's room and grabbed her and put her head under the covers so that she could not see him with blood all over his face. I was thinking that if I was in my daughter's room he would not harm me in front of her, but NO! He charged in the room and took his right hand and smacked me so hard on the left side of my head and face, that my eardrum rung. He busted my left eardrum and I screamed to the top of my lungs because it hurt so badly. I just held my daughter tight and did not fight or go looking for him, after he left her room. He soon left the house and got in his car, and drove to Mr. and Mrs. Haywood's house two hours away.

    The next day approached, Sunday morning, my husband had not returned home. I began a spiritual fast and prayer the night before. I was so devastated about my marriage and life so I went to church to have a little talk with Jesus. After church, I talked to the minister that started our marriage counseling that we did not complete. The minister agreed to speak to me and my husband, as soon as possible. I repented and was ready to talk to Nick about forgiveness and getting our house straight. I thought that by the time I got home, he would be at home or at least would have called his wife. I did not call and talk to anyone at this time, not even my mother because I'm married, embarrassed and devastated that my husband is mistreating me to this extent. I believe when you are married, you keep your marriage business in your home and you never tell anyone anything negative about your spouse. I believed that God was going to get us through the rough patch of our marriage, since we were still newlyweds in the process of becoming one.

So when I get home, Nick had not returned yet. I called him and he did not answer his phone. So I called my in-laws house to see if he was there. Mrs. Haywood answered the phone. I was respectful and spoke to her. I said, "Is Nick there? I have tried to call him but he is not answering." She replied in anger and rage, "Can you blame him? He got a gash on his head! I don't like what you are doing to my son. You hide behind that church and you don't pay your bills. You don't clean your house and all you want to do is shop." I replied, "When is Nick coming home because we are going to counseling and it's always three sides: my side, his side and the TRUTH. What does my bills and house have to do with you? As long as I don't ask you for anything and don't live with you, you shouldn't have anything to say to me. I'm a grown woman and you are being disrespectful." She hung up the phone in my face.

Up until that point in my life, I could not recall ever getting a whooping or being hit by any man. I also had not been verbally abused. Of course, my daughter had never seen any of this type behavior in her life. I prayed and did not know what to do. All I want is to get along with Nick and for him to love me. If he would treat me like a queen, I would treat him like a king. I prayed and cried out to the Lord, "Why we can't get along?" I'm willing to do whatever it takes to make my marriage work, since I married till death do us part. My trust has been violated. I live by a house of rules like a child. I can't continue with my dream career. We have been cursing and fighting against Gods will. Nick is calling his wife names of disrespect and belittlement without conviction and Shawn is being exposed to verbal and physical abuse in her home. On top of all of that, Nick's mother is a woman in agreement with her son's behavior. I lost all respect for Mrs. Haywood as a woman and mother- in- law. I felt like a failed mother and wife that was totally discouraged. Now you are telling Mr. and Mrs. Haywood, your side of the story, as if you are treating me like a queen. I had been telling them to come and help with the marriage before it got physical. I was reaching out to them for help and they never came to assist. They knew that their son was abusive and condoned me being mistreated. This was how we landed a great counselor at Trinity Counseling Center. He did not come home in time to meet the minister at church, due to Mr. and Mrs. Haywood saying, "He had to finish eating dinner before he returned home to his wife."

    I used to wreck my brain trying to understand Nicks thought process. But it all came out in marriage counseling after I used to call Mr. and Mrs. Haywood, expecting for them to come and sit down with us like civilized adults. The more I expected from his parents, the more I realized who the family that I married into really was. I never had a problem with telling the truth about any occurrences, but they always supported their son and I disagreed. I noticed he never would tell what he was doing in his home. People always saw my reaction but never the reason for my reaction. Mr. Haywood told Nick things such as:

- "You need to control her a**" (as if I was a donkey and not a wife with feelings)
- "She probably got a boyfriend" (something that was against my marriage and beliefs)

    His father always spoke negative against all my Christian beliefs as a wife. Why would a father- in- law plant a negative seed into his son's head, to make him think that his daughter- in- law had a boyfriend? That did not make any sense. I truly loved my husband and was depending on God to make my marriage work. I thought Mr. Haywood was disrespectful with the conversations he would have with me as a daughter in-law such as:

- "You like Church? I don't like church!"
- "I will be through eating by the time you finish all that" (as it pertained to saying grace)
- "You see how my wife sits there and don't say anything? That's what you need to learn how to do. You just married into the family see."
- One day, during a disagreement, my father- in- law called me a "crazy b***h." Again, my husband never defended his wife.

I thought Mrs. Haywood was disrespectful also:

- "You need to take your journals, burn them and start your life over. You would be a better person". She would check Nick's checking account since she worked at the bank. I felt that she is out of line and what mother checks a grown man's checking account. And we don't ask her for nothing we have our own money. Again, Nick did not say a word about her being disrespectful.
- "You go to that church and pay your money (tithes) to a church so that a preacher can drive around in a Mercedes"
- You are not going to Heaven
- You go to Bible Study but it does not help you

I was confused every time she responded to an email or talked to me. She would talk about church or my church attendance and tithes. She never discussed the issues that I was speaking of or understood that I meant no disrespect. She never had any resolutions to eliminate the drama and get to peace. Keep in mind, Mrs. Haywood never said five words to me in person. But over the phone and emails she was feisty for no reason. She never got to know me or hold a decent conversation with me because she did not want to. She would only stare at me and later during an email or phone conversation let her anger, for whatever reason, out on me. I did not even know that many words could come out of her mouth, until she was on the phone. After a while, I felt we needed to have an in person woman to woman talk and get to the bottom of the issue. I thought this would eliminate the constant disrespect and belittling conversations, but she did not want to talk. Truthfully, she just never liked me in my opinion. I didn't care if she didn't like me, because she never really got to know me anyway. After a couple of visits to her home, I began to feel sorry for her. She was always running around cleaning and doing laundry until she would get the okay from her husband to sit down, like she was a child. I soon put her on my prayer list as a woman. I had a dream like Martin Luther King, that one day me and my mother- in- law would get along, and have great conversation and do things together. That was far from her dream. I soon accepted the fact, that the family did not like me and I was not trying to please any of them. I never walked around with a Bible, quoting scriptures or forcing religious beliefs onto the family. How I lived in my house was all that mattered. My faith was tried on many occasions, and after conviction and repentance I would apologize. I could not change their hearts about how they felt about me. I could not believe a person, such as myself, that had a big, giving, caring heart brought so much anger and drama into a family. I wanted do whatever it took to be normal and get along. I wanted my husband to treat his mother better on Mother's Day. She is your mother and she should be the first person that you acknowledge on Mother's Day. I used to buy her cards and gifts, and give them to him to give to her. He would wait until the last minute or not do anything for his mother at all. This is a true sign about a man that does not treat his own mother the way that you want him to treat you. We are all saved and believers but could never get to peace according to God's word. It was always confusion and me trying to get along.

    I prayed, fasted and cried about this to my husband. He never cared about the same things that I cared about: family, morals and values. After a pattern of apologizing for different occurrences,

I noticed I was the only one that would apologize and move on. They would still be holding grudges and mad about old stuff that I had totally forgot about. I was like God wakes us up every day with a brand new mercy, and we are still mad about stuff that happened a month ago. We were held hostage to past occurrences, which kept us as a family bound to the past. This stopped us from moving forward. But keep in mind that we all are Christian believers according the family with different beliefs. But why couldn't God eliminate the drama? After all, if I let them tell it I'm crazy and the start of all this drama. But I'm the only one that wanted peace and to please the Lord with my mouth and actions. I encourage all married couples to keep your business in your home, and please share nothing about a disagreement or misunderstanding, without both parties present. Honestly, don't share anything at all with the parents.

Of course, after he went to his parent's house and talked about me while he was mad it made matters worse. We came from different types of parenting, whereas my grandparents or parents would have tried to bring us together and talk to us to make amends and get along. It's important to know how the other families thought process is prior to marriage. You don't want to disrespect your spouse's mother, but at a certain point in the relationship, you should expect for your spouse to protect you from disrespect even if it's from his family. That is a sense of security and protection that a spouse should provide to his wife.

The first time I left him he had a temper tantrum and screamed through the phone, "YOU LEFT ME! YOU LEFT ME!" He was acting like an abandoned child. He was younger than me and still in his twenties when we got married. He was still under his parent's wing and not mentally ready for the responsibility of marriage. Mr. and Mrs. Haywood never fully let the eaglet soar on his own so when real life events occurred in the marriage, all Nick knew was to call home to his parents. I had been on my own since I was 19 years old, and had been a single mother for ten years. I had accomplished almost everything on my own as a single mother. Parents are great and grandparents are wonderful, but it's a line of demarcation that has to be established during a marriage so that two people can become one.

What mature adults and grandparents condone such foolishness? The marriage did not have any family support from his parents to get to peace. But he always had family support from my family. They never judged him. They knew he needed a personal relationship with Jesus to feel convicted of his behavior. To this day, my spiritual mother says, "He is going to be an awesome man of God one day", because she knows the power of prayer.

My family always loves without judging and even when they know he is wrong, Nick knows they will love him regardless and he can call them anytime. My family believed in counseling and therapy but I'm not too sure that Nicks family new of the benefits.

I began to get angry about marriage. I would say "I HATE BEING MARRIED" and "I HATE MY LIFE." I began to live a married life thinking my own husband hated me. My marriage felt like the enemy's camp and I no longer wanted the marriage, even if God was to fix it. I could not share much with my husband because he was not my friend, and always made me feel like something was wrong with me. If I said," I had a rough day at work." He would respond and say, "The job ain't the problem the problem is you!" I wanted to attend dental school. I had an entrepreneur mindset and could not see myself working for anyone for the rest of my life. In dentistry, the chances of getting the dream career with benefits and retirement were slim to none while working for someone else, in my opinion.

I began to go to counseling on my own and work on my healing from all the disappointment. It was very obvious my husband did not like me. I began to battle with low self-esteem, which I really never had an issue with before. If we went somewhere, he was never happy to be with me. He wouldn't hold my hand or dance with me. All I wanted was affection and to be in love with my husband. It was hard to be affectionate and sexually available to my spouse. After a while, cursing became the norm in the home and church attendance was never for my husband. I would get upset and mad every Sunday since I had to go to church alone. I wanted to attend the marriage classes at the church and fellowship with the other couples whom I'm sure had a testimony. As a man, he never discussed what I desired to make me happy as a wife. I soon stopped working in ministry at the church to avoid the embarrassment of my marriage and I felt as if dental school was far away. We were married but living single lives and spiritually disconnected. I wondered to myself if I was to ever have a tragic accident would he take care of me. If I could not speak for myself would he make sure he spoke the right things for my sake. He always wished harm or bad on me so I did not want to live the rest of my life with someone I did not trust to have my best interest at heart.

I began to contact the police every time there was a disagreement for the overall safety of my home. I called the police because I never knew how he would react, because the norm for him was verbal abuse. I was trying everything I could for him to love me. He still would do harmful things to me and never see his wrong. You see when two are arguing and fighting, you don't know who the fool is. But when one stops and the other person is performing all alone, he knows he is the fool. So I stopped fighting and decided that I did not want the marriage anymore.

I continued to pray that God would release me from this daily turmoil and misery. Soon, Nick began to fight battles alone with no response from me. I could truly say I was done with the marriage and nothing in me wanted it at all. I was planning a way of escape since the first time I applied for divorce he was served papers while I was still living in the home with him and that was a huge mistake. I was thinking that if you are so miserable with me, why don't you leave me and get a divorce? I was thinking that he would agree it's time to call it quits, so we can get to a place of peace. I was so tired of not getting along with my husband. I wanted to be in love. I desired for my spouse to love and appreciate me. I started fantasizing about a new husband and being treated worthy, gentle and kind. For I knew, love conquers all!

One day, I cried my last tear and God released me from my marriage. I know that God does not like divorce and I tried to make it work as we entered into our third year. Nick was arguing with me about holding my son and watching him. He was so controlling and wanted to think for me. I couldn't even tell him I don't want to hold the baby. He was able to crawl or go into a walker, but Nick insisted that I hold him. I began to feel very depressed and was praying about the spirit of depression not coming over me. So Nick was demanding that I hold the baby. I was walking away from him and he was following me, and trying to throw the baby into my arms. As I went up the stairs, he followed me and I went down the stairs, he followed me. I had my house clothes on and would sleep with my keys in my bra, just in case, I had to escape suddenly. I did not want to fight or argue. I just wanted him to leave me alone. Suddenly, he put the baby down and wrestled with me, throwing me over the couch onto the hard wood floors. I got up and ran into the garage, and hopped into my car quickly, locking the doors. As he began to charge at me with a shovel, I backed my car out the garage and drove off as he hit the hood of my car with the shovel. I drove off and went to the gas station nearby. He got physical because I didn't want to hold the baby. He treated me like I was his child telling me what and how to do things. I prayed that I had some coins in my car to use the pay phone to call him. I said, "Are you okay? Are you done with your temper tantrum?" He replied "Yes" and that he had called the apostle's counselors to come to the house. I said, "Okay, I'm on my way home. If you are okay, I have not touched you and I don't want to fight." I went home and did not say a word to him as I went upstairs to take a hot shower. I got dressed and sat on the couch waiting for the apostle's counselors. He looked at me and said, "Are you okay?", as if he did not just come at me with a shovel. The apostle's counselors came to the house to speak with us at the kitchen table. They asked him why he came at me with the shovel and he responded nonchalantly, "I don't know." He had no remorse for what he did again, as if he did nothing wrong. I got my release from the Lord to leave my abusive marriage that day. The plan of escape was in process. I started to ignore the family and barely went around, once I knew that I got my release. Again, I'm thinking that if we get a divorce, everything can go back to normal. I can be happy alone like I was prior to marriage, and the family can go back to the way they used to be prior to me coming into their life. I now realized this man that I married did not have the qualities that I liked or needed as a woman.

He would threaten me by saying, "If you ever leave me, I will try to destroy you". But I didn't care. I knew that Jesus was going to take care of me. My mind used to remember him telling me confidently, "God ain't gone help you", of course you have to consider the source. God said, "Try the spirit by the spirit, and don't be conformed to his thinking. I have a proven track record with you. You know I will help you." I stood on a scripture, Psalms 119: 59, which says, "I thought about my ways, and turned my feet to your testimonies. I made haste, and did not delay to keep your commandments." He said you will be able to witness for yourself Psalm 119: 71-72 "It is good for me that I have been afflicted, that I may learn your statutes. The Law of Your mouth is better to me than thousands of coins of gold and silver." I can truly understand loving and praying for your enemies in spite of how you feel now.

So we were still seeing a counselor, and I shared with her I did not want to work on the marriage any longer. I felt she never listened to what I wanted or needed. I felt she was so focused on trying to save the marriage, and have me live in turmoil daily. I got to the point I could not sleep at night. She referred me to a psychiatrist about the depression. The psychiatrist listened to me explain the drama and "the shovel situation" was the last straw of the behavior. She too wanted me to get to a place of peace. I informed her that I was leaving and was prepared for whatever he shall bring my way. I explained how controlling he was and how he explained he would destroy me. I shared with her that my grandfather had gone to glory, and missing him had begun to affect me daily. I shared with her that I sat in my closet mourning and crying over my grandfather, and how close we were. I told her that my husband really hurt me by saying, "All the death in world does not justify how you act." And that my grandfather was a very important man and role model in my life. I shared with her about my biological father dying and I also lost his father, my other grandfather shortly after. She said, "It's possible you could have post-traumatic stress disorder and it's important to get to a healthy environment." I had not slept in days, so she gave me some samples of sleep aids and medicine to help me relax through the process. I prepared to leave the house and get an apartment. I tried to talk to him about the divorce process or possibly a legal separation. He refused to talk about it. I explained to him when I was leaving and that I was okay with taking whatever he let me have or take with me. I did not want any drama over stuff. I just wanted to leave and be in my own space safely. I was done with the drama after the shovel incident. I was terrified.

When the movers came, he decided I couldn't have certain things that I needed. I just said, "Okay, no problem", and the movers began to get mad at him for treating a woman the way that he did. I said, "God will provide", and kept it moving because I was getting closer to peace since I could sleep at night now. I got an apartment in close proximity to the house, so we both could still be in our son's life and take him to school. I had not totally decided to file for divorce due to finances and I knew he would give me a fight. I was thinking let's have some time apart and maybe do a legal separation, until we can discuss important matters such as our son who was about 2 years old at the time. When I got to the apartment I was relieved to be in my own space. The next morning, as I prepared to get dressed for work, I realized my pants had a hole in them. It was a perfectly nice hole on the pants leg. I went into my closet and to my surprise, he had cut all my work clothes with a pair of scissors as they were hanging on the hanger. I was tired of him and happy for peace, I just shook my head.

What women need from husbands:
Love, affection, support, security, protection, friendship, understanding, spiritual guidance, parental comfort for the kids, kind words that uplift and not tear down or discourage, peace, and most of all great communication skills along with many more that you could add that are positive.

Things you should know prior to marriage:
1. Do both of you have the same beliefs?
2. Do you and the family get a long? (since you marry him and the family)
3. Have you discussed having kids?
4. Are you best friends?
5. Does he have morals and values?
6. Do you know who you are in Christ?
7. Do you know who's you are that you belong to Christ?
8. Is he supportive of your beliefs and career dreams?
9. Is he insecure?
10. Does he have trust issue?
11. Has he accepted your past and past relationships?
12. How is the relationship expected to change after marriage?
13. Are you considered his property once married?

The person I married was the same person during the 6 months of dating. He just never let his true colors show and camouflaged himself to get what he wanted from me. My friends used to say, "He was everything you needed him to be to get you." The police had been called to our home over 20 times in three years. He was only arrested once for domestic violence. I had suffered a broken right hand as a result of us fighting like cats and dogs. During our marriage, we had destroyed laptops, drove a car through the garage door, and wasted money on repairs to the home monthly from fighting, damaged cars, reputations, careers and friendships. He would talk about me to the neighbors, and not just one, but all the neighbors on the block. He would say things about me that were not true and just always talked about me to destroy my character. The other wives would tell me what their husbands told them. I would feel embarrassed, and at the same time feel sorry for my husband. I always felt something was wrong with him. I just wished that I had his families support to get to the bottom of the issue. But they never thought anything was abnormal, or mutually agreed to dissect the behavior of their Nick.

So this chapter is not to add to or subtract to what I did in the relationship. Regardless, of how saved I am, I'm also human. It's always a cause and effect, an action and a reaction to whatever situation you are in. But most of all, it's a RIGHT AND WRONG way that a man is to treat his wife and children. A woman should never fight a man or think that she has the right to put her hands on him. Verbal abuse and physical abuse should not be tolerated from anyone. You don't have to react to every situation. Walking away is the best defense and revenge is not necessary. The Lord will fight your battles. No More Drama by Mary J Blige, Papers by Usher, and Blame it on me by Chrisette Michelle, were the songs that helped me get through the hard times.

Remember:
- The truth will go further than a lie.
- It's better to leave the relationship than to destroy each other.
- Your kids have little eyes and ears and they see and will do what you do. Watch what you expose your children to in the home.
- Your home should be your peace haven where you feel

secure from the world.
- Love conquers all!

Sometimes you are already equipped for the storm and have no idea. The praise and worships you deposited over the years are stored away in a savings for the storm. When you see me, please understand that nobody did it but God. Greater is He that is in me than He that's in the world. I would not take anything away from my journey.

I encourage all to seek God and Godly counsel when making life decisions or facing events. And don't ignore the signs. They are real.

I sought God's word, and His word confirmed that my drama is not a flesh and blood fight. You stop losing your witness and acting like a devil. You are guilty as well when you try to hurt the person that is hurting you. I want you to start speaking love, regardless of how you are treated. Remember hurt people hurt other people. Nick was already like this prior to marrying you.

God said, "Get to a place of peace and release, so you can embrace your new beginning." You need to establish and declare that everything you endured or have done is in the past and give thanks to God that you are free. What the devil meant for your bad, worked out for your good. With an exhale and sigh of relief you can scream, "IT'S OVER!"

Chapter 5
IT'S OVER

I used to have a friend that would listen to my boy problems. Fortunately, she has been with the same guy since high school and is happily married to him. She has NEVER and I repeat NEVER experienced the drama I have experienced related to dating and/or relationships. But she was always a listening ear and gave me advice. She had that one saying that was sure to come out of her mouth, during every situation, "When you get sick and tired of being sick and tired, let me know." I don't think I ever in my past mentally got to that point, until I experienced the biggest mistake of my life by marrying the wrong person. I was literally sick and tired of being sick and tired, and I wanted the nightmare to end. It would be nice if when a break up occurred both parties would agree to go their separate ways. For this to occur there needs to be a mutual understanding that it's not going to work. Unfortunately in most cases, due to soul ties and emotions it's one person that just can't let it go. I have been guilty of that myself in my life when a boyfriend would break up with me and I wanted the relationship more than anything. No one likes rejection and I totally understand that. It's a difference in a breakup if you are the one doing the breaking up versus the one who will be hurt by the breakup. The person that wants to break up usually has no concerns or hurts related to the matter. As I sat back and looked over my life, when someone had terminated the relationship and didn't want to talk to me anymore I remember the actions I portrayed and performed. The constant calls only to go to voicemail and leaving a message never to be returned. I would drive by their house just to see if there was new car around or in the driveway. Back in my younger days, I even went as far as to burst all four tires on a man's car. I also sent an email or letter in the mail just to express my feelings and concerns, but knowing it was not going to change the matter. Basically, I was holding on to something that in the other person's mind was over!

So I decided to leave the family. I was wishing that it could have been a mutual agreement based on the facts. We were not happy and we were both destroying each other in front of our kids. I knew that God was not pleased. He said, "I'm going to get the divorce papers". I was okay with that. I was thinking there is no reason why we both can't agree to go our separate ways. Then the drama began when I moved out.

1. Once I got to my apartment I found that all of my work clothes had been cut up.

2. I separated our phone accounts and the phone company accidentally cut his phone off. He thought I did it on purpose. I have no reason to cut your phone off, after all we have to discuss our son.

3. So he started changing the settings on my phone. I kept getting alerts that changes had been made to my account. I would call the phone company about this and they would put security information on my phone. Later, I found out that he requested my phone log and paid $200 for it. He began to call every number in my phone.

4. A week after I moved out I started getting calls from people stating that my husband had contacted them. So, of course I called him upset as well as called about our son.

5. He stated he was going to file for divorce and I would get

the divorce papers. I was waiting for the papers, and to my surprise one night at 3 am, I heard a bang on my apartment door from a sheriff. Nick had filed a restraining order on me for harassment. Why had he not filed for a divorce instead of a restraining order? I had no idea. When I would call him about my son, he would say that he was going to file a restraining order on me. But I knew that I was not harassing him and did not want the drama. When he came to court I noticed that he was with his dad Mr. Haywood. I had a strong feeling that Nick loved me, but did not know how to express his self or his feelings. This was based off of his example from Mr. Haywood. Mr. and Mrs. Haywood controlled my marriage and Nick and they tried to control me. I was over it that day. I filed for a divorce the next week, even though I could not afford it at the time. I can just file for a divorce and we can move on. We don't have to harm each other.

  6. I sent a spiritually encouraging email to everybody in my email contact list including him. I failed to bcc, so he took it upon himself to email everybody that was attached to my email. He degraded my character and reputation. He said I was sleeping with men that were on the email. Male friends that were my friends from high school and college. My kid's teachers were attached to the emails and he lied stating that Shawn wanted to run away from home etc. So, of course the school contacted me and inquired.

  7. He took our son to the doctor every time he had him after my visitation, alleging that I was doing something harmful to our son. He was trying to build a case against me to show me as an unfit mother.

  8. He contacted my job and would harass the other employees if they said I was not there. He would say, "I know she's there" etc. It was escalated to my manager, who then referred me to the employment services for counseling related to stress.

  9. He had my car picked up by one of his friends with a tow truck. I was then informed that a tracker had been placed on my car. When I called him about my car he said, "Your car is the

number one most stolen car in America", implying that it had been stolen.

10. Nick withdrew our son from his school one day. So when I got to the school I was informed that he did not attend school there on a regular basis. Of course, as a mother I started calling and sending emails in order to find an answer. Due to the dynamics of Nick, I knew that he would try to destroy me if I went to his house. He would file a restraining order if I kept calling. This situation forced me to go back to court. I did not find out where my son was until I went to court and the judge asked Nick where the baby was. The judge explained that the divorce was not final and he could not take the baby out of the county. He informed the courts that our son was in Watkinsville, GA. I thought to myself "Where is that at?" He was trying to push my buttons so that I would react in anger and do something that I would regret. You know as a mom we will snap, but we have to be mindful of how the enemy works and how he lives to steal, kill, and destroy. He will use what is close to you, like your kid.

11. He would come to court and make up lies to prolong the divorce and drag it out. He would say mean stuff that was far from the truth and make statements like my kids have been in DFCS, and that I was mentally unstable. This caused the courts to have to investigate and make additional court appearances.

12. He asked me to bring our son some clothes one day. I needed a file cabinet from the house, so I asked for it. When I got to the house I rang the doorbell. He opened the door as my son stood in the doorway and threw my mail on the ground, instead of handing it to me in my hand. He slammed the door without giving me the file cabinet. So I pulled my car into the driveway since I was on the opposite side of the street. I went and rang the doorbell again. Soon, the police arrived, stating that he called the police on me for blocking him in the driveway of our house.

He has called the police on me falsely for kidnapping my own son. He moved two hours away, in an effort to diminish me and our son's relationship. Our phone conversations went from one extreme to the next, so I decided to be more cautious. After a phone call we had one day, he stated, "You deserve to go to jail for calling the police all the time". I called the police every time I did not know what state of mind he was in, and after all, he did not have a great balance mentally.

Again, what did I do that was so bad that this person was angry during marriage, angry when I filed for the divorce and during the divorce. What did I do that in his mind I deserved to be mistreated and mentally destroyed by lowering my self-esteem. What did our kids do to deserve to be is such a hostile environment daily?

Don't do anything you will regret or that will bring harm to your life. It's not worth it. I have learned "everything understood does not have to be discussed". Ladies the best advice is to let it go and don't say anything. Silence is golden, especially when a soul tie is attached. Out of the heart the mouth speaks. You don't want to speak out of emotions and hurt feelings. You may say something you will regret later and cannot take back. If your children hear it they will then do it as a form of learned behavior. As seasoned women of wisdom say, "If you can't say anything nice, don't say anything at all". Mrs. Haywood said to Nick during a verbal abuse altercation. "That's how you was raised but you know it isn't right." I was like WOW! As I repeated what she said to me? How do you expect him to do what's RIGHT when you raised and taught him what is WRONG? What a disconnect!

You see the news and people are killing each other over a relationship, and then selfishly leave the kids behind. You actually never know what occurs to get a person to the breaking point of insanity. You always hear the same lines, "He/she was so sweet and worked with the community, had a giving heart, was nice looking and smart". They look just like you and me on the outside, but on the inside they have unresolved issues of negative emotions, and unhealed hurts from the past that never got addressed. The tie that causes you to make wrong decisions can also cost you a possible life time of regret. As I'm writing this chapter, the news reported today "A Kansas City Chiefs football player, shot his wife then drove to the stadium and shot himself, leaving behind a 3 month old baby. He just signed a 1.9 million dollar contract in 2009." It appears he was very successful because of his career, and they mentioned his money to let you know, he was financially well off. The news showed a family photo and they appeared to be happy. Remember, we see the outer part. We don't see his past or the depth of his soul. We don't see if he was a controlling man or had insecurities. We don't know if he was healed of his past hurts or attended counseling after a tragedy in his life. All I can think is how selfish he was to leave a 3 month old baby without his parents, due to your uncontrollable emotions. It takes me back to my close friend, Mia Reid, whom was shot and killed in front of her 10 year old daughter in 2008. Her ex-fiancée did it inside of a Baton Rouge Apartment. I can't imagine taking someone else's life, and leaving children without a mother or father. I also have another mother and female friend who faced tragedy earlier this year. In Kansas City at the Royal's stadium, a boy called his girlfriend to the car and as she approached the car he shot her a couple of times, placing her in the intensive care unit. When it is over it is over!

As people, we have to accept when it's over and move on to healing; and not another person to try to suppress the pain. After a breakup, I'm guilty of saying, "I'm just going to occupy my mind and time with somebody else". "If I just get with somebody else, I will get over him quicker". "I'm going to have a drink". I would look in my phone or black book, and contact people I know I don't want to talk to. But because I'm hurt, I'm searching for a pain reliever in all the wrong things, people and places. None of that would have healed my heart, or broke the soul tie to prepare me for another mate. Now when you meet another guy, you are not giving him the real you, healed and unconfused. It is selfish to meet an innocent person and have them pay for the pain of your past. Every time a separation occurs you must take a break to gather your thoughts and feelings before entering into another relationship.

After my divorce, I was really focused on me. I met some people and I did not know how to say no without being rude, I literally would have to tell them to leave me alone! Even males that considered themselves a friend started to invade my private time. I used my alone time as a moment of reflection and healing, but men would meet me and rush me to spend time with them. I was focused on me and thought that respectfully, we could just be friends. But later, I realized it was all hidden agendas to possibly date me. I felt they did not respect my time and I should not have to explain to any man where God has me at this point of my life. I have experienced men being distractions in my life and reflected on all the time I wasted. I had personal goals that I had not achieved and placed them on the back burner due to a man. I was totally confident with myself and where I was going in my life. I finally understood how a man can be a distraction.

I'm finally in love with my relationship with Jesus. I have a sense of peace in my life, and doing what the Lord has for me to do in this season of my life. Women just because a man wants to go out and date you, please don't allow what he wants to determine what you need. If he loves Jesus, he will respect your time and Jesus' timing as well. Enjoy your "me time" after a separation and embrace that you are a single woman again. I wish men knew that not all women are running around looking for a mate. Some of us are comfortable in our own skin. I love being a single woman and I'm going to focus on me and if I feel that you are a distraction, then you have to go. Ladies don't hold on to anything. Ladies, I encourage you not to make the same mistakes I made. When it's over for you and you are ready to move on, I want you to say this prayer:

"Lord, I thank you for waking me up this morning, in my right mind to make right decisions. First, I want to repent and ask for forgiveness of all the wrong things I did, even the things that I'm not aware of. Clear my heart and soul from all unrighteousness please renew in me a clean heart. Make my thoughts and my spirit pure and whole again. I come to you as humble as I know how, asking for a supernatural miracle, healing and a breakthrough. Destroy the yoke of bondage connected to me. Allow me to forgive others and value who I am in Christ. Please allow me to accept the things that I cannot change. I have accepted the breakup and that it's over. In Jesus name, Amen"

Now you have experienced the breakup, you have accepted it and prayed for forgiveness, it's time to focus on the breakthrough. You don't ever want to convince someone to stay with you and be in denial of the state of your relationship. When I look back over my life and all the breakups I had, I realized I'm still where God wanted me to be, even though I took a detour. Never hold on to what God has already separated you from. I encourage single women to practice abstinence and/or celibacy, to develop a pure state of mind and establish the right type of relationship through discernment. You have to be very cautious, of whom you come in contact with, and allow in your space. Get comfortable in your own skin and define yourself. Don't allow a man to define you and your value. It's okay to cry and wallow in pain, but only for a little while. "I can do anything for just a little while".

God only needs one tear to dissect with a microscopic lens to formulate the right ingredients for your healing and breakthrough. He only needs one tear. Embrace the fact that "IT'S OVER!" No more growing up in the church or playing church. Embrace "it's over", to avoid crying out "OH MY GOD! WHAT A MISTAKE!"

Chapter 6
IV-Giveness

Forgiveness is such a serious concept in a person's spiritual walk and future. You must understand that God has already forgiven you, so you have to forgive yourself. Once you have forgiven yourself then you can forgive the other person. Here are four steps that one must do to begin the process:

- I-   Accept God's Forgiveness
- II-   Forgive Yourself
- III- Forgive Others
- IV-   Operate In Total Forgiveness

<u>Accept God's Forgiveness</u>
In our Christian walk, we have a relationship with the Father that is like no other relationship that can be compared to across mankind. God is so sovereign that He wakes us up every morning with brand new mercy and grace. He has given us the opportunity to freely accept a personal relationship with Him. He allows his

children to have a spirit of conviction when we are wrong. That spirit of conviction means that you are human and acknowledge you're wrong. God will convict his children and he will forgive you at the same time. He allows you the spirit of repentance when you are wrong and he forgives you, regardless of your faults or shortcomings. He never judges you or holds you hostage to your past. I'm so appreciative of the Father's forgiveness because it allowed me to start a new day, and live a new life of abundance. It does not matter if people don't forgive you. What matters most is that God forgives you. You should become a "God pleaser" and know that He has already forgiven you for your past mistakes. Some people don't acknowledge their mistakes or even know that they need Jesus. You're definitely a child of God when you can come to the throne of grace with humbleness in your heart and say, "I made a mistake and I need you Lord".

Forgive Yourself

Most times forgiving yourself is hard. This is because you have high expectations of yourself to please God and you are worried about what people may think or say. Being able to forgive yourself comes from knowing who you are according to God's word. When you know who you are, there is no human being that can control your thought process to sway you in a mental level of defeat and discouragement. It doesn't matter when you did it, how you did it, if it was wrong or right or the biggest mistake of your life. God has already forgiven you so you can forgive yourself and know that all things, good bad and ugly work together for them that love the Lord. He will never forsake you or leave you stranded alone without a way of escape. I was so miserable in my marriage and the only person that was there with me was the Lord. God is so omnipotent and omnipresent in our lives. When I decided and contemplated divorce, I would battle with the fact that God does not like divorce and I had to stay because I don't want to displease God. But I was hurting and confused about love, and God said to me, "You are

my child, I have forgiven you and you must forgive yourself". God did not want his child or children mistreated and abused. God does not rejoice in your pain and disappointments. I prayed to God daily about staying and making my marriage work, according to the word and God's plan. I received a release from the Lord to leave the marital home and pursue a legal separation. I expected for Nick to come with open arms of regret and humbleness, and say, "I'm sorry, I love you and my family. I want to make this marriage work to maintain a family". I felt that was what I deserved and the children deserved, as I prayed for it daily. God said, "Don't focus on what he does. Focus on me and what I'm about to do".
God said since I have forgiven you and you have forgiven yourself, before I develop you and transition you into your new beautiful life, I require two things of you. Forgiving others and operating in total forgiveness resembling a heart that is pleasing to the father. Don't act on what you see or hear. You should act on what you know the word declares about you. I forgave myself of unrighteous behavior and looked forward to being free to forgive others, according to God's standards.

<u>Forgive the others</u>
Since Nick is the father of my child, I forgave him. I never wanted harm to come on him. I love him as my child's father but don't like his ways or character. I actually wanted him to find another woman, after a certain point in time, so he could be happy. I felt that since he was so unhappy with me and I have all these faults, then just leave and be happy with someone else. Prior to every court appearance, I would pray and stand on a scripture. I wanted to forgive Nick for myself and begin my healing process soon. I had wasted too much time operating in the flesh and not the spirit. He was like an enemy to me, and the word says to love your enemies. I realized loving your enemies is the hardest thing to do. It's really rough when your enemy is the one you should be joined with until death do you part. It's even rougher when you have a little innocent

child in the midst.

I stood on the book of Daniel, while I was going through my divorce, and maintained my focus by wearing a pair of red shoes every time I went to court. It was an ugly divorce, so ugly that I had anticipated writing a book entitled OMG! What a Divorce. But it is so important that you know who is ultimately in control during any process of your life. God is always in control behind the scenes, even when you can't see it. I was assured that the God I served was mighty in battle, and that no weapon formed against me was going to prosper. I felt that our son needed both parents in his life regardless of our personal issues within the marriage. Neither one of us is considered the perfect parent. But who is? Every parent does the best that they can, with what they have to the best of their knowledge. My husband was coming to court with all types of tactics and lies to find a reason for me never to see my son again. How do you maintain your focus on the Lord in battle? You wear a pair of red shoes. You have to maintain your focus or you will sink. Think about the story when Jesus asked Peter to walk across the water and he informed him to maintain his focus on the Lord or he would sink. So I wore a pair of red shoes every time I went to court to remain calm and focused all while ignoring the schemes and distractions of the enemy.

His lies were the worst lies a husband could ever say about his wife. For example, he stated that I slept with our neighbor in the back of a truck and he had it on videotape. So I asked to watch the videotape to entertain his lie. The tape never showed up because it was all lies. Then he would persuade people that his lies were true. I got so used to him making up lies in our marriage that I would just shake my head during the divorce. One day one of the neighbor's wives came to my house to tell me something that Nick said about me. I told her, "Lady, just pray for him because I can't keep up with my husband's lies. Use it as entertainment and please don't come tell me anything ever again."

So the heat was getting hot in court with lies and defeat, I was standing on Daniel and my faith was huge like Shadrach, Meshach, and Abed-Nego. I refused to worship foreign gods and worship anything that they did. But how many of you know that the bond between a mother and a son is one of the strongest parental bonds, and it can't be broken no matter what. It's a totally different feeling of protection from the world, which a mother expresses for her son. "If that is the case, Our God whom we serve is able to deliver us from the burning fiery furnace, and He will deliver us from your hand, O king" (Daniel 3:17). Of course, some people like to drag the courts and children through the divorce process, out of hurt and anger. That is unfortunate because the children suffer, when you have to spend time and money in court to try to prove a pointless situation. In between court appearances, Nick would take our son to the doctor allegedly saying I had done something harmful to our son. Then he would file a motion to eliminate my entire visitation until the divorce was final, but it was not granted because it was lies and tactics that he made up. Now I remember my grandfather saying, "The truth will go further than a lie." It was so true during this time of my life. I could not keep up with the lies in court, and of course, I could never keep up with them during the marriage.

    I prayed about the divorce process because he always threated to do harmful things to me if I ever left him. If I made it through years of marriage with the dysfunctional behavior, I'm sure I can make it through a divorce. But I failed to pray prior to the divorce, about my son and how he would be affected. I cried daily about my poor son and the drama that was constantly going on around him at such a small age during the divorce. My son was 2 years old and Shawn was 13 years old. Shawn understood more than my son due to his age. Every time he was with me during the divorce, he would just hold me so tight and kiss me all day. I was thinking if he was away from me for a long period of time he would forget me and not know who I was. Then I remembered the unbreakable bond between a mother and child.

I began to seek the Lord about my son and the divorce process, and how this would affect him in the long run. I expressed to God how I felt about Nick and our son. I said, "God I would give anything to have my father and grandfather in my life at this time. Time is so precious and I believe that it takes a man to raise a man in today's society. I agree that Nick needs some more maturing in his life, as it pertains to manhood. But I believe with time maturity will come and that time heals all wounds. I believe that hurt people hurt people, and they don't care who they use in the process. I see that Nick is using our child to hurt me and I have to make a decision on the process towards forgiveness. I don't have any problems with him as a provider, but I refuse to tear him down in court because I'm hurt. I want to be honest with myself. I want a divorce but I never want our son to be in a position where he does not have both parents. Our son deserves both parents participation in his life, even though the marriage did not work."

God said to me, "You are blessed to have a man that wants to raise his son, even though his motives are wrong. I pray that you know I have great plans for you as a mother." I heard the voice of the Lord say, "Let it go, stop killing your children with all this fighting. You have to be the bigger person and you are a child of the king. Release and start your process of forgiving your ex-spouse, his family and anyone that will prohibit you from conquering your destiny." To finalize the divorce, I signed a settlement agreement in court for joint legal custody, allowing Nick to be primary parent and raise our son as the primary gaurdian. I did not want Nick to be bound to large child support bills monthly. I felt and knew that he would always provide for our son. I also knew that our son was the first grandchild for Mr. and Mrs. Haywood and that being exposed to both parts of the family is important. I didn't want anything but a divorce and to raise our son together, regardless of our differences.

Since I was raised by my grandparents, I feel that it's important for grandparents to be of assistance if the parents are in need. But never should they take the sole responsibility of either one of the parent's role. As a child I used to wonder why my mother was not present for certain things. As I got older I realized how much my grandmother took over as a parent and never allowed my mother the full responsibility of parenthood. I would hate for my son to get older and experience the same thing. I feel this way because Nick allows the grandparents' role to supersede my role as a mother. I broke a generational curse in our family by raising my own daughter. Nick, as primary parent and out of hurt, moved our son two hours away after the settlement agreement was signed to be raised by Mr. and Mrs. Haywood. Rightfully so he can move, but out of respect he should have discussed the move with me and as a parent he should have made sure I understood his plans, prior to signing the settlement agreement. Again, I'm expecting a conversation to take place out of respect. Unfortunately, he legally separated me from our son and only allows me to have visitation according to the court documents. For anything pertaining to our son he asks Mr. and Mrs. Haywood since he refuses to communicate with me as a parent. So our innocent son has to be raised by third party grandparents. They take him to school, pick him up, take him to the doctor, and to get haircuts etc. The move has diminished a relationship between mother and son. On some of the legal documentation my name is not even mentioned. I used to pray that the Mr. and Mrs. Haywood would eliminate themselves from the equation so that Nick would have to communicate with me regarding our son. That is a never ending battle since they have always been so involved with the marriage, the divorce, and now the raising of our child. Nick gives them more rights than he gives me as a mother, because he is primary parent. So even though we are divorced, the child is still used as a source of control over me in order to inflict hurt. He has never respected me as a woman and does not respect the fact that we have joint legal custody. It's a never ending financial battle in court and again Nick and Mr. and Mrs. Haywood never see anything wrong with the situation.

But I still have to forgive them, even though they don't know the importance of a mother in a child's life. The situation with my child has got to work out for my good. I know that God told me to sign the settlement agreement and allow Nick to be the primary parent. So what does God want to do with me? What is he birthing inside of me? I know He did not bring me through all of this hell for nothing.

I went to the "Night of Vision" at Word of Faith in 2012. I was truly blessed, when Minister White was on the microphone jamming with the word of God. I was hype and feeling everything she said about purpose and destiny. I immediately heard the voice of the Lord. And He informed me through a minister that it was my time to pursue my purpose and personal goals, regardless of how much time I had lost and past failures. She said, "God's final decision is his original plan" and "What you make happen for others, God will make happen for you." The original plan was for me to go to dental school prior to meeting Nick. I knew that was my purpose and desire. God said to me, "It is still your purpose and desire. I have set you up for such a time as this. Take advantage of being the secondary parent while pursuing your purpose, passion and goals at the same time. You have not lost your son. It's all going to come together after a while". I love the Lord when he speaks to me through the man or woman of God's preaching.

During my session with Jack A. Daniels, I shared my thoughts and journals that I had compiled during this rough season of my life. I had always contemplated a book in my spirit and wanted Jack's opinion. He mentioned this book was my release and I began to focus on my book. I made up in my mind that in 2013 I will not deal with any drama from Nick. All I want is results. I put it in my promise jar as a reminder. In the beginning of the year I received phone calls and text messages that could have been alarming to the "unforgiving" Mica. I have been able to dodge fiery darts and pass tests that were placed in front of me. I feel deep in my heart that Nick always loved me. He just did not love me the way that

I understood love to be. For a mother to allow her two year old baby boy to be raised by his father as the primary custodial parent with joint legal custody is not only forgiving the person, but most importantly it is the beginning of operating in total forgiveness.

Operating in Total Forgiveness

You have to operate in forgiveness in order to maintain a healthy lifestyle for your children if you have a child by the person that you have to forgive. You must establish boundaries and operate by a system to help you maintain your character in a hostile situation. At some point in the relationship you understand that this person does not receive information well from you so you can never persuade that person to think like you and vice versa. Do what you can as a person, even when it's not received by the other party. Never give up on establishing the operations that you have put in place. Remember God is working on a situation even when it does not look like it. The most important thing is the children seeing how you operate in love and forgiveness. Even the little children that are two and under have a spirit of discernment. They can tell when things are not right within an environment with the parents. They have little eyes and little ears that absorb everything. So establish your operation system to get to peace and maintain a healthy environment after the divorce or separation. Look for the good in every bad situation. Realize that you are not the only person that has been through a tragedy and been misunderstood. The best is yet to come, so look forward to your future and enjoy your freedom as a born again Christian. As I was going through my situation with Nick in the court system of Fulton County, GA, I had some divine encounters with people. I always wanted the relationship and situations that occurred to make sense to me. I used to pray daily to the Lord about the lack of misunderstanding that I had. Again, I was loving to him and supportive and at any given time when he was ready to operate in love and get to a healthy environment for the children, I was ready. I had strong beliefs that were established in my childhood. Love your neighbors, don't curse in the home or period, always support your spouse, your home is your peace haven, you are to leave and cleave from the parents, etc. I wanted my home and environment to be like that or at least close without the drama for the health of my family. I met a woman over the phone one day when I did not know what to do and where to turn. I decided to contact the domestic violence lines that are given in court for support. I wanted the divorce to end and stop dragging out. I explained that I'm married and that my spouse just mistreats me and does not want a divorce. She asked if I could contact his family and get support. I explained that I have reached out to the family, and sent emails in the past to help him and the situation, but they refuse to help him. She began to ask me questions and listen more to the situation over the phone. Remember, I never met this woman in person, it was a divine encounter over the phone. After a while, I felt like I was in a counseling session over the phone. She ended the call and said, "Please go get this book as soon as possible. Read it and it will help you to understand what you are going through and how to get to peace." I was like okay I have read every book in America. What could be so special about this book? She said the name of the book is "WHY DOES HE DO THAT? INSIDE THE MINDS of ANGRY and CONTROLLING MEN", by Lundy Bancroft.

 I immediately went to purchase the book and began to read it. It was a page turner and it was the life I had lived for the past 4 years. I was so amazed that someone really could relate to the behavior and thought process that I had to deal with. I was so pleased that a book was published to help me understand the madness. The book was the foundation and assistance I needed to learn how to move on and get to a sense of forgiveness. The book helped me understand why Mrs. Haywood never helped me escape from Nick or showed sympathy towards me when the abuse would occur. I was able to finally forgive Mrs. Haywood for not defending me when Nick gave me a whipping like I was a child. Mrs. Haywood was mad at me when I defended myself. She could not understand. I had never been hit in my life by a man, cursed out, nor been played with through mind games. I'm able to operate in total forgiveness with her and pray for her daily as a woman. Women should always support each other from any form of abuse. I know that a mother knows their child and I will never condone my children's misbehavior. I was always ready to have a decent conversation or meeting of the minds with Mrs. Haywood during the marriage. She was never accepting of that and never initiated any effort to get to a sense of understanding with her daughter-in-law at the time. She just made up excuses for Nick as if he was a child stating, "He is not a morning person. He never saw his dad hit me. I don't know where this is coming from. You know you were raised with cursing in the home, but you know it's not right." I expected more from a woman, regardless of that being her son, because of all the womens rights that we fought for over the years.

When you understand the way a person was raised, and the thought process behind what they do, it helps you get an idea of the type of person you are dealing with. You can make better decisions on how to respond or react. It used to be said that for every action is a reaction. I have learned that for every action, sometimes people expect a reaction based on your past experiences. Be cautious of things that are planted for you to react to. The other party wants to get a rise out of you. These things can be used against you and the other party will never show what they have done. The only thing that will be visible is your reaction. The main things that have helped me operate in total forgiveness are:

First, having a personal intimate relationship with God. It's necessary for the foundation of your daily Christian walk. I seek to please Him daily in all my actions and everything that I do. He is in control.

Second, I'm standing on a word—"But the fruit of the Spirit is Love, Joy, Peace, Longsuffering, kindness, goodness, faithfulness,

23gentleness, SELF_CONTROL. Against such there is no law. 24And those that are Christ's have crucified the flesh with its passions and desires. 25If we live in the spirit, let us also walk in the Spirit. 26Let us not become conceited, provoking one another, envying one another." (Galatians 5:22).

Third, remember that today you are a new creature, and the people that you have forgiven are new creatures also. Everyone wakes up every day with brand new mercy and grace. So old things are passed away and your future will be greater than your latter. Remember forgiveness is a process and Success is the sum of small efforts. Repeat it everyday.

"You don't have to tell everyone your entire history. Just know that Jesus calls, on purpose, women with a past. He knows your history, but He calls you anyway" (New King James Version-Holy Bible, Women Thou Art Loosed! Edition T.D. Jakes)

My Bishop once stated, "Wisdom is learning what to ignore." During your journey of operating in total forgiveness, you will begin to ignore a lot of things and maintaining self-control will help you accomplish this, when the other party has not begun to forgive. Forgiveness will take you on a path of deliverance. The very thing that oppressed you will be used to elevate you; it will deliver you from Egypt to the promise land. Problems to provision, don't ever give up on your dream. That dream will serve as a bridge, in the middle of the fire, you will not be burned. He delivers thoroughly and completely. Don't give up on your dreams. The very thing that tried to kill you, becomes the subject matter for your own book.

Ladies, Parents being too involved in marriages and not respecting you as a wife will destroy your marriage. People only do what you allow them to do in your marriage. Get a man that understands the concept of leave and cleave and his parents understand it as well. "For this reason a man will leave his father and mother and be united to his wife, and the two will become one flesh." (Ephesians 5:31). But if he is a Godly man he will know how to protect his wife as the head of her life. Parents will destroy your marriage if you allow it.

It's important that I mention that this book is not about Mr. or Mrs. Haywood or anyone other than me. It's about the decisions that I made constantly, until I made the biggest mistake of my life by marrying a man against God's will. I knew this to be true since we were unequally yoked with different family values, morals and beliefs. Now the "light bulb" is shining bright in my life. I understand why Jesus says to marry a person that you are equally yoked with. I understand why Jesus does not want us to fornicate. Especially when it can result in raising a child with one parent teaching righteousness and the other parent teaching mess. It results in a child being possibly confused between right and wrong. Jesus never wanted a mother to raise a child alone or experience a soul tie that is why he did not want sex outside of marriage. It all makes sense now that I have made those mistakes.

For my son's sake, I pray for me and the ex-family's relationship daily. My prayer is that the transparency that is demonstrated, throughout the book, is used for the building up of God's kingdom. I also pray that Christian ladies will use this book as an example to make better decisions related to marriage to avoid experiencing anything other than what the Lord has for you. His blessings are "yes" and "Amen". I operate in total forgiveness knowing that God is ultimately in control and has the last word regardless of what it looks like.

Chapter 7
#1stLOVEFoCuS

Even though, God has given you so many chances and forgiven you so many times; you don't want to be in a position to have to ask him for forgiveness again related to a similar relationship. You want to make the right decision on love and relationships, so that God gets all the glory. Now that you're focused on pursuing your first love all over again, in a deeper way, you can shout, "OH MY GOD! JESUS, Thank you for loving me and my MISTAKES!"

God clearly will sit you down and deal with you one on one. He sat me down as his child, saying the following:

"I told you not to marry that man, but you went according to your plan and your clock. If you would have waited for me, you wouldn't have had to deal with the drama or pain. I told you when you went to college, if you would have listened to me, you wouldn't have had a child out of wedlock. I told you that if you would seek my face, I would direct your path. But I accept you with open arms to come back to me, and I will love you like you never made a mistake and went astray. I love you so much. I will return to you everything that you lost. I will make sure you know who you are and whose you are, because my love for you has never failed or changed. It remains the same.

I'm the same God yesterday, today and forever more. No one

voted for me to be God. I did not say choose me, I will make a good God. Any one that chooses me shall have everlasting life forever and ever, Amen. I said all of your requests are 'yes' and 'amen'. You are the apple of my eye. I brought you with a price and I gave my only begotten son so that you may have life and life more abundantly, but you chose to go the other way. I'm a kind God. I don't force myself on you. I wait until you come to me with heartache, pain, soul ties, verbally abused, mentally confused, hurting and all alone. So when you come to me, I bring you out pure as white snow, without a blemish. So that you can say nobody did this but God. You will not give any body the credit for what only I have the power to do, change and heal.

I will prepare you for your mate daily at this intimate season of your life. I will prepare you to love like you've never been hurt. I will teach you agape love. It's a process to greatness, and after this, you will be great and greater than before. You will know that I'm first in your life. All you need is a God fearing man and the rest is settled in heaven. Don't be concerned about finances, but be focused on what I say about finances. I know where you are now and what your credit score looks like. Prepare yourself to be pursued with your focus on me, and the mate I have for you will seek after you. He will see your glory and your presence will light up a room. He will see you and know you are sent from the Father. It's a man that finds a good thing. That man will obtain favor from me and you will be the helpmate that he needs to conquer all of his God given goals, dreams and aspirations. He will know he is blessed and will cherish you as God's precious vessel.

Your career will be what you desired for it to be, out of obedience to Me. Ears haven't heard and eyes have not seen the good things that I have in store for you. They tried to destroy you, but they can't destroy what my spirit rest, rules and abides in."

God told me that I have a testimony to share with other women in college, which are battling with sex and ruining their careers. God also told me, "Go help them so they don't make a mistake. You have single women that desire to be married because they feel their clock is ticking. Go help them so they don't make a mistake. You have high school girls that need to know abstinence makes sense, so they don't make a mistake. You have a testimony to allow many women to know that you have never seen the righteous forsaken, or his seed begging for bread. They are already whole. All they need is a mate that has his own anointing to help them taste better. They already are a loaf of bread all by themselves, and I will send the butter to anoint them. He will be the head and covering over their life to lead them into the path of righteousness".

Ladies, God is honored when you came to pursue your first love in a deeper more intimate way. He has looked into your tears with a microscope to make sure he develops the right cure for you to come and get it right with him. He put special ingredients and people in your path to lead you to him at this point and season of your life. He has set you up to be blessed and to get you on the track and the path that you are on now. Your ladder will be greater as you stay focused on him and his path. Don't go to the left. He has some promises waiting on you and it's crucial that every second of every minute you stay tuned in to him and your purpose. You are about to walk in purpose towards your destiny.

The moment that God told me to birth a book, it was the beginning of a purpose driven journey towards my destiny. After all of these events, in this book, I return back to my first love at 35 years old. Not that I ever left him, I was just walking my own path ahead of him without any guidance, sometimes leaning on my own understanding. I look back over my life and wonder how it would be, if I would have stayed on the path that Jesus had for me.

What I do know is that mistakes happen when I'm on my own path and not God's path. Now in my new life, I want to see what God's path is all about. I want to make sure I run this race without getting weary. He has placed some "sold out" Christians in my life, I can see the fruit they bear. So I know it's sweet and good. I'm running on to see what the end is gone be on God's time, on God's path, with God's instruction and direction. He is my compass and "your word is a lamp unto my feet and the light unto my pathway." (Psalm 119:105). So God dealt with me and allowed me to pour everything in me out into this book. My new life is filled with purpose and the things that I desired in my old life, as it relates to a mate, are not the same in my new life.

I remember going to conferences as a single woman, and most women wanted a man with a six figure salary. It's fine to have a six figure man. What are you going to do when the money runs out or a tragic event occurs in your marriage that money can't buy? What about a man that does not know how to give you the love and affection you need as a woman? All he knows is how to buy you things and you want what money can't buy, a simple hug. A woman should not be dependent on a man's finances to determine if he is a good man or not. I have seen so many women that have put their all into a man for years and assisted with his career goals and when he got to the top he left that woman. She had no place to go and had not worked a job in years. She felt it was too late to go to school and get her own career because she wasted so much time on him. I'm here today to tell you as a woman, if you fit this category, please pursue your career and God given purpose. Your life is not over because he left you and walked out on you. If you pursue your first love, He will allow you to walk towards your future and erase your past.

As I began to pursue my first love, I heard a conversation that Marshan Evans shared on 860AM ChatKafe.com. She spoke and a light bulb was turned on in my spirit. She talked about a breakup and a moment of silence where she just listened. I felt that was confirmation at that moment, for me to birth my book and pour out of me what is in me. It was the beginning of my brand and release of stuff that was built up inside of me that I wanted the world to hear. I went to a Mrs. Right seminar around the same time with Tony Gaskins, and he spoke about the 3 B's: Brain- Brand- Body. I already had the body because I'm very cautious about my appearance and weight. I love to go to the gym when I have time. He talked about the brain which I already had and at the time was preparing for dental school. But when he talked about the brand, I was like hmmmm... thinking scratching my head. This book was already in me and I already had a title and words written on paper. I have no idea about writing a book and how to put it together. Then a friend said, "Just write and pour it out of your spirit". So with this book, I wanted to give you me poured out, nothing fancy. What I have experienced was not fancy or cute, there wasn't anything nice about it and so many women have a voice and a story. I felt like mine needed to be heard. Out of all the women in the world surely I can help somebody. I have a heart to give and help people.

I felt I did not have any soul ties and if I did this book as a release that would heal any unknown soul tie. The release of this book has helped remove any hurt and a memorial stone can be buried. Make up in your mind to birth what is inside of you. Get a plan for your life with God leading the way.

I have started to invest in my future by pursuing my first love, which is loving and developing me. One of the revelations I received is that you can't do it alone, and may need assistance rebounding from previous failed relationships. Some key areas and people that played an important role in my process of starting over are:

1. My life coach, Jack A. Daniels, the author of Stay Out of Your Own Way, I Need a Wife and many more. I think it's important to have someone to talk to that is results driven. If you need direction on where to go with your life have a "Shot of Jack" at *www.presspause.org*

2. Philanthropist, Jennifer Lester who is affectionately known as the "Self Help Queen", is a psychotherapist, life coach, motivational speaker and author of '14 Ways to Find Your Amazing: When passion and purpose collide'. *www.thepurposeproject.com*

I began to focus on me, my kids, and dating Jesus. I want to date with a purpose and not date on purpose. I realized that no matter how much I find a man attractive, I need to wait on God and be receptive to His will. I always thought to myself, well the men that I like don't like me, and the men that like me I don't like them. I had to get myself in a position to be pursued by the men that I like. I redeveloped some of my character flaws. I have noticed as I pursued my first love, God has taken some stuff out of me that I did not like, and he put some new stuff in me that I liked. Jesus changed my ingredients and cooking temperature, as preparation for my divine mate. Jesus will purge us of some stuff and store it away.

My desire is to be more in love with Him daily. We have an intimate relationship so deep, that after I hear his voice, a sense of peace rocks me to sleep. Our time is very valuable and we both are valuable to each other.

One day Jesus came to me and talked to me about my value, and relayed to me that I was "his pearl" and "his diamond". He talked about the pressure that diamonds endure to be perfected, and the pearl inside of the oyster. He related it to my past and how I was in a perfecting state, for such a time as this.

God's Pearl:

You are Gods pearl, experience how intimate your relationship is with him, and put your name in place of mine so you can experience Gods encouraging words speaking to your soul.

He said, "Mica you are my pearl. You are hard but soft on the inside. I made you hard so you could be bulletproof, and anything that is shot your way would not destroy you. So you are aware of the fiery darts that the enemy tries to bring your way in an effort to separate you from me. You are soft on the inside, so that you're aware of your feelings when they get hurt, and you will know you have a soft heart that can resemble love regardless. I never want your heart to be hardened. That will prevent you from showing the love of Christ. It's a heart thing! Love conquers all".

"You are an ideal pearl usually perfectly round and smooth, but many other shapes of pearls do occur. I made you smooth, so if words come up against you, they can roll off your back like a duck. The different shapes you resemble are merely you being able to fit into whatever environment I shall bring you in. And you are not in a square box. You can be shaped into God's image to do the work of the kingdom. You are highly valued as an object of beauty. Embrace your beauty and how I made you wonderfully and fearfully unique. No longer do I want you to look at your beauty as a curse. I made you wonderfully and fearfully unique. Who shall you fear? When you are more beautiful on the inside than the eyes can see".

"You are something rare, fine, admirable, and valuable. You are so valuable to me, I wrote a popular book called the Bible, to remind you of who you are to me. You are the apple of my eye and I admire you more than anybody on the earth. It is rare that you will find the same love I have for you on earth. The most valuable pearls occur spontaneously in the wild. When you couldn't see the forest from the trees, I saw you amongst all the forest and trees and rescued you my pearl out of the wild and wilderness. Mica, you are my pearl and my diamond, because you were developed under irritating pressure at high temperatures. Only a diamond or a pearl could have gone through what you went through, and come out as pure, ready to pursue your first love and focus on me. When you think you have made every mistake possible, I will use your mistake for the building up of the kingdom. All the counseling that you went through will benefit you in the future. People that seek help know they need help and find it. Be concerned about the people that don't even realize that they need help".

Its okay to focus on your first love in the meantime with an expectation of your God sent mate.

Since, he will be sent by God, he is fully equipped with the armor you need to be the head of your life. He will be healed of soul ties. He will know who he is and whom he belongs to. He will be sensitive to the Holy Spirit and your needs and concerns as a woman. He will speak words that up lift and not tear you down verbally. He will know what real love is because God will be his first love. He will lead you closer to Christ then to himself. He will accept your children as his own. You will walk together in unity equally yoked on one accord to conquer the world of God's kingdom. Wake up daily looking forward to the day God sends him your way.

    In the meantime, I'm waiting patiently like a whole loaf of bread with all the right ingredients baking in the oven, until Jesus' timer goes off indicating: SHE'S READY! I pray to God that I never have to say, "OH MY GOD! I MADE A MISTAKE AGAIN".

Chapter 8
TESTIMONY

After 5 years of operating in total forgiveness, time healing all wombs and falling in love with your 1st love you are like a caterpillar ready to become a butterfly as the transition to a beautiful life becomes a reality. Hurting people hurt people, so it's important to allow the healing process to occur. While you are in a storm or post-divorce you may feel that healing will never occur. Going through a divorce is so emotionally, financially and mentally draining on all parties involved the kids and family included. It is a death that occurs without a funeral. It is saying goodbye to we and us to hello to me. It is at times separating a tie that can never be tied again. It can end in not only divorce but everything that comes with it possibly short sales or foreclosure of a marital home, changing last names, bank accounts and funds to possible having to file bankruptcy and credit being ruined. It can also involve hurt and/or angry kids that resent one if not both of the parents. It can involve ex-in laws and their emotions to the separation of family bonds and family time during holidays. It is a lot of moving forces and can be depressing to endure such change and pain. It is at these moments when you have to pull all your strength from the Lord. Because "He gives strength to the weary and increases power to the weak". Isaiah 40; 29

But then God shows up in the mist of all the adversity and begins to restore hearts, minds and souls for all individuals involved ready to receive. It's not instant at all its like one day your walking along and it hits you and you think to yourself WOW we just had a cordial conversation for the first time in years. It makes you think to yourself and ask was it me or him that changed. Or did we both decide to just let it go? Did we heal from the pain and hurt? You just start questioning yourself and smile saying there is a GOD. If it was not for the many tests in our life we would not have a testimony. God is so faithful and is still in the miracle working, restoration business and changing situations and people every day. But first he will change you!

As the girl in the red shoes was healing God was changing her heart and allowing her to see things from the perspective of others. Especially towards her ex-in laws Mr. and Mrs. Haywood. Remember when she said this "I used to pray that Mr. and Mrs. Haywood would eliminate themselves from the equation so that Nick would have to communicate with her regarding their son." Well that all changed because her perspective changed and she realized the African proverb "It takes a village to raise a child" And for a child to have as many opportunities he/she could with his grandparents to make memories is a blessing and life changing. In order for the situation to change she had to change the lens she was looking through regarding the relationship. As God was restoring the relationship between her and Mr. and Mrs. Haywood Nick began to see their relationship blossoming and sarcastically would refer to them as best friends and/or BFF's. With everyone getting along Nick soon came around and became cordial. He was so nice that she didn't realize he was the same person that she married 7 years ago. It just takes time and people change so of course they are not the same people that they married.

At times your faith is tested and you wonder when will this season change and/or pass away? And then seasons change and people change situations and circumstances change. In life you never know who you will need or what life may bring.

After time, as fate would have it the divorcees transitioned into a beautiful life. Co-parenting and enjoying birthday celebrations together with both sides of the family for the child to see a healthy relationship between his divorced parents. Their able to respect each other's new relationships and operate as if they were never hurt. Only GOD Can Do That! The statement "Time Heals All Wounds" is true. The smoke is clear, hearts are healed and healthy communication can now take place even after a Mistake.

I'm a witness, two people can co-parent, raise their son in a healthy environment and truly experience peace after the storm of a crazy divorce. "And we know that all things work together for good to them who love God, to them who are the called according to Gods purpose." Romans 8; 28

No matter how many mistakes you make God is still there to bring you out without a blemish. He did it for the three Hebrew men thrown in the fiery furnace and continues to this day. Our trials come to make us strong, but it is hard to believe that or understand it while in the storm. Prayerfully we gleam and learn while transitioning our mind to operate as a renewed spirit daily. As you get stronger in your faith, your prayer life increases and you become more resilient to trials. It's impossible to predict how long a trial will last. Can you imagine the red sea walking path ditch used by the Israelites was 9miles and 300 feet deep? That's an example of how we can focus on the problem and how long it will take to reach our destination or choose to trust God during the journey. But as children of God we are not destined to walk in mud, rocks and or ditches we are designed to walk in the best. Get your red shoe focus on the destiny, the lesson and the process to a greater YOU! Focus on God, not the problem and/or the unpredicted outcome regardless of your Oh My God, Mistakes

Made in the USA
Columbia, SC
03 June 2019